By Robert Lowell

Land of Unlikeness (1944)

Lord Weary's Castle (1946)

The Mills of the Kavanaughs (1951)

Life Studies (1959)

Phaedra (translation) (1961)

Imitations (1961)

For the Union Dead (1964)

The Old Glory (plays) (1965)

Near the Ocean (1967)

The Voyage & Other Versions of Poems by Baudelaire (1969)

Prometheus Bound (translation) (1969)

Notebook 1967–68 (revised and expanded edition, *Notebook*, 1970)

History (1973)

For Lizzie and Harriet (1973)

The Dolphin (1973)

Selected Poems (1976) (revised edition, 1977)

Day by Day (1977)

The Oresteia of Aeschylus (translation) (1978)

Collected Prose (1987)

Collected Poems (2003)

The Letters of Robert Lowell (2005)

Selected Poems (2007)

Life Studies

AND

For the Union Dead

Life Studies

AND

For the Union Dead

ROBERT LOWELL

FARRAR, STRAUS AND GIROUX

NEW YORK

Farrar, Straus and Giroux
18 West 18th Street, New York 10011

Printed in the United States of America
First published in 1967 by Farrar, Straus and Giroux
This paperback edition, 2007

Library of Congress Control Number: 2007929093
Paperback ISBN-13: 978-0-374-53096-9
Paperback ISBN-10: 0-374-53096-3

www.fsgbooks.com

20 19 18 17 16 15

Contents

Life Studies

For the Union Dead

Life Studies

For
ELIZABETH

Part One

Part One

Beyond the Alps

(On the train from Rome to Paris. 1950, the year Pius XII defined the dogma of Mary's bodily assumption.)

Reading how even the Swiss had thrown the sponge
in once again and Everest was still
unscaled, I watched our Paris pullman lunge
mooning across the fallow Alpine snow.
O bella Roma! I saw our stewards go
forward on tiptoe banging on their gongs.
Life changed to landscape. Much against my will
I left the City of God where it belongs.
There the skirt-mad Mussolini unfurled
the eagle of Caesar. He was one of us
only, pure prose. I envy the conspicuous
waste of our grandparents on their grand tours—
long-haired Victorian sages accepted the universe,
while breezing on their trust funds through the world.

When the Vatican made Mary's Assumption dogma,
the crowds at San Pietro screamed *Papa.*
The Holy Father dropped his shaving glass,
and listened. His electric razor purred,
his pet canary chirped on his left hand.
The lights of science couldn't hold a candle
to Mary risen—at one miraculous stroke,
angel-wing'd, gorgeous as a jungle bird!
But who believed this? Who could understand?
Pilgrims still kissed Saint Peter's brazen sandal.
The Duce's lynched, bare, booted skull still spoke.

God herded his people to the *coup de grâce*—
the costumed Switzers sloped their pikes to push,
O Pius, through the monstrous human crush. . . .

Our mountain-climbing train had come to earth.
Tired of the querulous hush-hush of the wheels,
the blear-eyed ego kicking in my berth
lay still, and saw Apollo plant his heels
on terra firma through the morning's thigh . . .
each backward, wasted Alp, a Parthenon,
fire-branded socket of the Cyclops' eye.
There were no tickets for that altitude
once held by Hellas, when the Goddess stood,
prince, pope, philosopher and golden bough,
pure mind and murder at the scything prow—
Minerva, the miscarriage of the brain.

Now Paris, our black classic, breaking up
like killer kings on an Etruscan cup.

The Banker's Daughter

(Marie de Medici, shortly after the assassination of her husband, Henri IV. Later, she was exiled by her son and lived in a house lent to her by Rubens.)

Once this poor country egg from Florence lay
at her accouchement, such a virtuous ton
of woman only women thought her one.
King Henry pirouetted on his heel
and jested, "Look, my cow's producing veal."

O cozy scuffles, soft obscenities,
wardrobes that dragged the exchequer to its knees,
cables of pearl and crazy lutes strung tight—
O tension, groin and backbone! Every night
I kicked the pillows and embroidered lies
to rob my husband's purse. I said his eyes
flew kiting to my dormer from the blue.
I was a sparrow. He was fifty-two.

Alas, my brutal girlish mood-swings drove
my husband, wrenched and giddy, from the Louvre,
to sleep in single lodgings on the town.

He feared the fate of kings who died in sport. . . .
Murder cut him short—
a kitchen-knife honed on a carriage-wheel.

Your great nerve gone, Sire, sleep without a care.
No Hapsburg galleon coasts off Finisterre

with bars of bullion now to subsidize
the pilfering, pillaging democracies,
the pin-head priest, the nihilist grandee.
Sleep, sleep, my husband. There at Saint Denis,
the chiselled bolster and Carrara hound
show no emotion when we kiss the ground.
Now seasons cycle to the laughing ring
of scything children; king must follow king
and walk the plank to his immortal leap.
Ring, ring, tired bells, the King of France is dead;
who'll give the lover of the land a bed?
My son is adding inches in his sleep.
I see his dimpled fingers clutch Versailles.
Sing lullaby, my son, sing lullaby.
I rock my nightmare son, and hear him cry
for ball and sceptre; he asks the queen to die. . . .
And so I press my lover's palm to mine;
I am his vintage, and his living vine
entangles me, and oozes mortal wine
moment to moment. By repeated crime,
even a queen survives her little time.
You too, my husband. How you used to look
for blood and pastime! If you ever took
unfair advantages by right of birth,
pardon the easy virtues of the earth.

Inauguration Day: January 1953

The snow had buried Stuyvesant.
The subways drummed the vaults. I heard
the El's green girders charge on Third,
Manhattan's truss of adamant,
that groaned in ermine, slummed on want. . . .
Cyclonic zero of the word,
God of our armies, who interred
Cold Harbor's blue immortals, Grant!
Horseman, your sword is in the groove!

Ice, ice. Our wheels no longer move.
Look, the fixed stars, all just alike
as lack-land atoms, split apart,
and the Republic summons Ike,
the mausoleum in her heart.

A Mad Negro Soldier Confined at Munich

"We're all Americans, except the Doc,
a Kraut DP, who kneels and bathes my eye.
The boys who floored me, two black maniacs, try
to pat my hands. Rounds, rounds! Why punch the clock?

In Munich the zoo's rubble fumes with cats;
hoydens with air-guns prowl the Koenigsplatz,
and pink the pigeons on the mustard spire.
Who but my girl-friend set the town on fire?

Cat-houses talk cold turkey to my guards;
I found my *Fraulein* stitching outing shirts
in the black forest of the colored wards—
lieutenants squawked like chickens in her skirts.

Her German language made my arteries harden—
I've no annuity from the pay we blew.
I chartered an aluminum canoe,
I had her six times in the English Garden.

Oh mama, mama, like a trolley-pole
sparking at contact, her electric shock—
the power-house! . . . The doctor calls our roll—
no knives, no forks. We file before the clock,

and fancy minnows, slaves of habit, shoot
like starlight through their air-conditioned bowl.
It's time for feeding. Each subnormal boot-
black heart is pulsing to its ant-egg dole."

Part Two

The account of him is platitudinous, worldly and fond, but he has no Christian name and is entitled merely Major *M*. Myers in my Cousin Cassie Mason Myers Julian-James's privately printed *Biographical Sketches: A Key to a Cabinet of Heirlooms in the Smithsonian Museum*. The name-plate under his portrait used to spell out his name bravely enough: he was Mordecai Myers. The artist painted Major Myers in his sanguine War of 1812 uniform with epaulets, white breeches, and a scarlet frogged waistcoat. His right hand played with the sword "now to be seen in the Smithsonian cabinet of heirlooms." The pose was routine and gallant. The full-lipped smile was good-humoredly pompous and embarrassed.

Mordecai's father, given neither name nor initial, is described with an air of hurried self-congratulation by Cousin Cassie as "a friend of the Reverend Ezra Styles, afterward President of Yale College." As a very young man the son, Mordecai, studied military tactics under a French émigré, "the Bourbons' celebrated Colonel De la Croix." Later he was "matured" by six years' practical experience in a New York militia regiment organized by Colonel Martin Van Buren. After "the successful engagement against the British at Chrysler's Field, thirty shrapnel splinters were extracted from his shoulder." During convalescence, he wooed and won Miss Charlotte Bailey, "thus proving himself a better man than his rivals, the united forces of Plattsburg." He fathered ten children, sponsored an enlightened law exempting Quakers from military service in New York State, and died in 1870 at the age of ninety-four, "a Grand Old Man, who impressed strangers with the poise of his old-time manners."

Undoubtedly Major Mordecai had lived in a more ritualistic, gaudy, and animal world than twentieth-century Boston. There was something undecided, Mediterranean, versatile, almost double-faced about his bearing which suggested that, even to his contemporaries, he must have seemed gratuitously both *ci-devant* and *parvenu*. He was a dark man, a German Jew—no downright Yankee, but maybe such a fellow as Napoleon's mad, pomaded son-of-an-innkeeper-general, Junot, Duc D'Abrantes; a man like mad George III's pomaded, disreputable son, "Prinny," the Prince Regent. Or he was one of those Moorish-looking dons painted by his contemporary, Goya—some leader of Spanish guerrillas against Bonaparte's occupation, who fled to South America. Our Major's suffering almond eye rested on his luxurious dawn-colored fingers ruffling an off-white glove.

Bailey-Mason-Myers! Easy-going, Empire State patricians, these relatives of my Grandmother Lowell seemed to have given my father his character. For he likewise lacked that granite *backcountriness* which Grandfather Arthur Winslow attributed to his own ancestors, the iconoclastic, mulish Dunbarton New Hampshire Starks. On the joint Mason-Myers bookplate, there are two merry and naked mermaids—lovely marshmallowy, boneless, Rubensesque butterballs, all burlesque-show bosoms and Flemish smiles. Their motto, *malo frangere quam flectere*, reads "I prefer to bend than to break."

Mordecai Myers was my Grandmother Lowell's grandfather. His life was tame and honorable. He was a leisured squire and merchant, a member of the state legislature, a mayor of Schenectady, a "president" of Kinderhook village. Disappointingly, his famous "blazing brown eye" seems in all things to have shunned the outrageous. After his death he was remembered soberly as a New York State gentleman, the friend and host of worldly men and politicians with Dutch names: De Witt Clinton, Vanderpoel, Hoes, and Schuyler. My mother was roused to warmth by the Major's scarlet vest and exotic eye. She always insisted that he was the one properly dressed and dieted ancestor in the lot we had inherited from my father's Cousin Cassie. Great-great-Grandfather Mordecai! Poor sheepdog in wolf's clothing! In the anarchy of my adolescent war on my parents, I tried to make him a true wolf, the wandering Jew! *Homo lupus homini!*

Major Mordecai Myers' portrait has been mislaid past finding, but out of my memories I often come on it in the setting of our Revere Street house, a setting now fixed in the mind, where it survives all the distortions of fantasy, all the blank befogging of forgetfulness. There, the vast number of remembered *things* remains rocklike. Each is in its place, each has its function, its history, its drama. There, all is preserved by that motherly care that one either ignored or resented in his youth. The things and their owners come back urgent with life and meaning—because finished, they are endurable and perfect.

Cousin Cassie only became a close relation in 1922. In that year she died. After some unpleasantness between Mother and a coheiress, Helen Bailey, the estate was divided. Mother used to return frozen and thrilled from her property disputes, and I, knowing nothing of the rights and wrongs, would half-perversely confuse Helen Bailey with Helen of Troy and harden my mind against the monotonous *parti pris* of Mother's voice. Shortly after our move to Boston in 1924, a score of unwanted Myers portraits was delivered to our new house on Revere Street. These were later followed by "their dowry"—four moving vans groaning with heavy Edwardian furniture. My father began to receive his first quarterly payments from the Mason-Myers Julian-James Trust Fund, sums "not grand enough to corrupt us," Mother explained, "but sufficient to prevent Daddy from being entirely at the mercy of his salary." The Trust sufficed: our lives became tantalized with possibilities, and my father felt encouraged to take the risk—a small one in those boom years—of resigning from the Navy on the gamble of doubling his income in business.

I was in the third grade and for the first time becoming a little more popular at school. I was afraid Father's leaving the Navy would destroy my standing. I was a churlish, disloyal, romantic boy, and quite without hero worship for my father, whose actuality seemed so inferior to the photographs in uniform he once mailed to us from the Golden Gate. My real *love*, as Mother used to insist to all new visitors, was toy soldiers. For a few months at the flood tide of this infatuation, people were ciphers to me—valueless except as chances for increasing my armies of soldiers. Roger Crosby, a child in the second grade of my Brimmer Street School, had thousands—not mass-produced American stereotypes, but hand-painted solid lead soldiers made to order in Dijon, France. Roger's father had a still more artistic and adult collection; its ranks—each man at least six inches tall—marched in glass cases under the eyes of recognizable replicas of mounted Napoleonic captains: Kleber, Marshal Ney, Murat, King of Naples. One delirious afternoon Mr. Crosby showed me his toys and was perhaps the first grownup to talk to me not as a child but as an equal when he discovered how feverishly I followed his anecdotes on uniforms and the evolution of tactical surprise. Afterwards, full of high thoughts, I ran up to Roger's play room and hoodwinked him into believing that his own soldiers were "ballast turned out by central European sweatshops." He agreed I was being sweetly generous when I traded twenty-four worthless Jordan Marsh papier-mâché doughboys for whole companies of his gorgeous, imported Old Guards, Second Empire "redlegs," and modern *chasseurs d'Alpine* with sky-blue berets. The haul was so huge that I had to take a child's wheelbarrow to Roger's house at the top of Pinckney Street. When I reached home with my last load, Mr. Crosby was talking with my father on our front steps. Roger's soldiers were all returned; I had only the presence of mind to hide a single soldier, a peely-nosed black sepoy wearing a Shriner's fez.

Nothing consoled me for my loss, but I enjoyed being allowed to draw Father's blunt dress sword, and I was proud of our Major Mordecai. I used to stand dangerously out in the middle of Revere Street in order to see through our windows and gloat on this portrait's scarlet waistcoat blazing in the bare, Spartan whiteness of our den-parlor. Mordecai Myers lost his glory when I learned from my father that he was only a "major *pro tem*." On a civilian, even a civilian soldier, the flamboyant waistcoat was stuffy and no more martial than officers' costumes in our elementary school musicals.

In 1924 people still lived in cities. Late that summer, we bought the 91 Revere Street house, looking out on an unbuttoned part of Beacon Hill bounded by the North End slums, though reassuringly only four blocks away from my Grandfather Winslow's brown pillared house at 18 Chestnut Street. In the decades preceding and following the First World War, old Yankee families had upset expectation by regaining this section of the Hill from the vanguards of the lace-curtain Irish. This was bracing news for my parents in that topsy-turvy era when the Republican Party and what were called "people of the right sort" were no longer dominant in city elections. Still, even in the palmy, laissez-faire '20s, Revere Street refused to be a straightforward, immutable residential fact. From one end to the other, houses kept being sanded down, repainted, or abandoned to the flaking of decay. Houses, changing hands, changed their language and nationality. A few doors to our south the householders spoke "Beacon Hill British" or the flat *nay nay* of the Boston Brahmin. The parents of the children a few doors north spoke mostly in Italian.

My mother felt a horrified giddiness about the adventure of our address. She once said, "We are barely perched on the outer rim of the hub of decency." We were less than fifty yards from Louisburg Square, the cynosure of old historic Boston's plainspoken, cold roast elite—the Hub of the Hub of the Universe. Fifty yards!

As a naval ensign, Father had done postgraduate work at Harvard. He had also done postgraduate work at M.I.T., preferred the purely scientific college, and condescended to both. In 1924, however, his tone began to change; he now began to speak warmly of Harvard as his second alma mater. We went to football games at the Harvard Stadium, and one had the feeling that our lives were now being lived in the brutal, fashionable expectancy of the stadium: we had so many downs, so many minutes, and so many yards to go for a winning touchdown. It was just such a winning financial and social advance that my parents promised themselves would follow Father's resignation from the Navy and his acceptance of a sensible job offered him at the Cambridge branch of Lever Brothers' Soap.

The advance was never to come. Father resigned from the service in 1927, but he never had a civilian *career*; he instead had merely twenty-two years of the civilian *life*. Almost immediately he bought a larger and more stylish house; he sold his ascetic, stove-black Hudson and bought a plump brown Buick; later the Buick was exchanged for a high-toned, as-good-as-new Packard with a custom-designed royal blue and mahogany body. Without drama, his earnings more or less decreased from year to year.

But so long as we were on Revere Street, Father tried to come to terms with it and must have often wondered whether he on the whole liked or disliked the neighborhood's lack of side. He was still at this time rather truculently democratic in what might be described as an upper middle-class, naval, and Masonic fashion. He was a mumbler. His opinions were almost morbidly hesitant, but he considered himself a matter-of-fact man of science and had an unspoiled faith in the superior efficiency of northern nations. He modeled his allegiances and humor on the cockney imperialism of Rudyard Kipling's swearing Tommies, who did their job. Autochthonous Boston snobs, such as the Winslows or members of Mother's reading club, were alarmed by the brassy callousness of our naval visitors, who labeled the Italians they met on Revere Street as "grade-A" and "grade-B wops." The Revere Street "grade-B's" were Sicilian Catholics and peddled crummy second-hand furniture on Cambridge Street, not far from the site of Great-great-Grandfather Charles Lowell's disused West Church, praised in an old family folder as "a haven from the

Sodom and Gomorrah of Trinitarian orthodoxy and the tyranny of the letter." Revere Street "grade-A's," good North Italians, sold fancy groceries and Colonial heirlooms in their shops near the Public Garden. Still other Italians were Father's familiars; they sold him bootleg Scotch and *vino rosso* in teacups.

The outside of our Revere Street house was a flat red brick surface unvaried by the slightest suggestion of purple panes, delicate bay, or triangular window-cornice—a sheer wall formed by the seamless conjunction of four inseparable façades, all of the same commercial and purgatorial design. Though placed in the heart of Old Boston, it was ageless and artless, an epitome of those "leveler" qualities Mother found most grueling about the naval service. 91 Revere Street was mass-produced, *regulation-issue*, and yet struck Boston society as stupidly out of the ordinary, like those white elephants—a mother-of-pearl scout knife or a tea-kettle barometer—which my father used to pick up on sale at an Army-Navy store.

The walls of Father's minute Revere Street den-parlor were bare and white. His bookshelves were bare and white. The den's one adornment was a ten-tube home-assembled battery radio set, whose loudspeaker had the shape and color of a Mexican sombrero. The radio's specialty was getting programs from Australia and New Zealand in the early hours of the morning.

My father's favorite piece of den furniture was his oak and "rhinoceros hide" armchair. It was ostentatiously a masculine, or rather a bachelor's, chair. It had a notched, adjustable back; it was black, cracked, hacked, scratched, splintered, gouged, initialed, gunpowder-charred and tumbler-ringed. It looked like pale tobacco leaves laid on dark tobacco leaves. I doubt if Father, a considerate man, was responsible for any of the marring. The chair dated from his plebe days at the Naval Academy, and had been bought from a shady, shadowy, roaring character, midshipman "Beauty" Burford. Father loved each disfigured inch.

My father had been born two months after his own father's death. At each stage of his life, he was to be forlornly fatherless. He was a deep boy brought up entirely by a mild widowed mother and an intense widowed grandmother. When he was fourteen and a half, he became a deep young midshipman. By the time he graduated from Annapolis, he had a high sense of abstract form, which he beclouded with his humor. He had reached, perhaps, his final mental possibilities. He was deep—not with profundity, but with the dumb depth of one who trusted in statistics and was dubious of personal experience. In his forties, Father's soul went underground: as a civilian he kept his high sense of form, his humor, his accuracy, but this accuracy was henceforth unimportant, recreational, *hors de combat*. His debunking grew myopic; his shyness grew evasive; he argued with a fumbling languor. In the twenty-two years Father lived after he resigned from the Navy, he never again deserted Boston and never became Bostonian. He survived to drift from job to job, to be displaced, to be grimly and literally that old cliché, a fish out of water. He gasped and wheezed with impotent optimism, took on new ideals with each new job, never ingeniously enjoyed his leisure, never even hid his head in the sand.

Mother hated the Navy, hated naval society, naval pay, and the trip-hammer rote of settling and unsettling a house every other year when Father was transferred to a new station or ship. She had been married nine or ten years and still suspected that her husband was savorless, unmasterful, merely considerate. Unmasterful—Father's specialized efficiency lacked utterly the flattering bossiness she so counted on from her father, my Grandfather Winslow. It was not Father's absence on sea-duty that mattered; it was the eroding necessity of moving *with* him, of keeping in step. When he was far away on the Pacific, she had her friends, her parents, a house to herself—Boston! Fully conscious of her uniqueness and normality she basked in the refreshing stimulation of dreams in which she imagined Father as suitably sublimed. She used to describe such a sublime man to me over tea and English muffins. He was Siegfried carried lifeless through the shining air by Brunnhilde to Valhalla, and accompanied by the throb of my Great Aunt Sarah playing his leitmotif in the released manner taught her by the Abbé Liszt. Or Mother's hero dove through the grottoes of the Rhine and slaughtered the homicidal and vulgar dragon coiled about the golden hoard. Mother seemed almost light-headed when she retold the romance of Sarah Bernhardt in *L'Aiglon*, the Eaglet, the weakling! She would speak the word *weakling* with such amused vehemence that I formed a grandiose and false image of L'Aiglon's Father, the *big* Napoleon: he was a strong man who scratched under his paunchy little white vest a torso all hair, muscle, and manliness. Instead of the dreams, Mother now had the insipid fatigue of keeping house. Instead of the *Eagle*, she had a twentieth-century naval commander interested in steam, radio, and "the fellows." To avoid naval yards, steam, and "the fellows," Mother had impulsively bought the squalid, impractical Revere Street house. Her marriage daily forced her to squander her subconsciously hoarded energies.

"Weelawaugh, we-ee-eeelawaugh, weelawaugh," shrilled Mother's high voice. *"But-and, but-and, but-and!"* Father's low mumble would drone in answer. Though I couldn't be sure that I had caught the meaning of the words, I followed the sounds as though they were a movie. I felt drenched in my parents' passions.

91 Revere Street was the setting for those arthritic spiritual pains that troubled us for the two years my mother spent in trying to argue my father into resigning from the Navy. When the majestic, hollow boredom of the second year's autumn dwindled to the mean boredom of a second winter, I grew less willing to open my mouth. I bored my parents, they bored me.

"Weelawaugh, we-ee-eelawaugh, weelawaugh!" "But-and, but-and, but-and!"

During the week ends I was at home much of the time. All day I used to look forward to the nights when my bedroom walls would once again vibrate, when I would awake with rapture to the rhythm of my parents arguing, arguing one another to exhaustion. Sometimes, without bathrobe or slippers, I would wriggle out into the cold hall on my belly and ambuscade myself behind the banister. I could often hear actual words. "Yes, yes, yes," Father would mumble. He was "backsliding" and "living in the fool's paradise of habitual retarding and retarded do-nothing inertia." Mother had violently set her heart on the resignation. She was hysterical even in her calm, but like a patient and forbearing strategist, she tried to pretend her neutrality. One night she said with murderous coolness, "Bobby and I are leaving for Papá's." This was an ultimatum to force Father to sign a deed placing the Revere Street house in Mother's name.

I writhed with disappointment on the nights when Mother and Father only lowed harmoniously together like cows, as they criticized Helen Bailey or Admiral De Stahl. Once I heard my mother say, "A *man* must make up his *own* mind. Oh Bob, if you are going to resign, do it *now* so I can at least plan for your son's *survival* and education on a single continent."

About this time I was being sent for my *survival* to Dr. Dane, a Quaker chiropractor with an office on Marlborough Street. Dr. Dane wore an old-fashioned light tan druggist's smock; he smelled like a healthy old-fashioned drugstore. His laboratory was free of intimidating technical equipment, and had only the conservative lay roughness and toughness that was so familiar and disarming to us in my Grandfather Winslow's country study or bedroom. Dr. Dane's rosy hands wrenched my shoulders with tremendous éclat and made me feel a hero; I felt unspeakable joy whenever an awry muscle fell back into serenity. My mother, who had no curiosity or imagination for cranky occultism, trusted Dr. Dane's clean, undrugged manliness—so like home. She believed that chiropractic had cured me of my undiagnosed asthma, which had defeated the expensive specialists.

"A penny for your thoughts, Schopenhauer," my mother would say.

"I am thinking about pennies," I'd answer.

"When *I* was a child I used to love telling Mamá everything I had done," Mother would say.

"But you're not a child," I would answer.

I used to enjoy dawdling and humming "Anchors Aweigh" up Revere Street after a day at school. "Anchors Aweigh," the official Navy song, had originally been the song composed for my father's class. And yet my mind always blanked and seemed to fill with a clammy hollowness when Mother asked prying questions. Like other tongue-tied, difficult children, I dreamed I was a master of cool, stoical repartee. "What have you been doing, Bobby?" Mother would ask. "I haven't," I'd answer. At home I thus saved myself from emotional exhaustion.

At school, however, I was extreme only in my conventional mediocrity, my colorless, distracted manner, which came from restless dreams of being admired. My closest friend was Eric Burckhard, the son of a professor of architecture at Harvard. The Burckhards came from Zurich and were very German, not like Ludendorff, but in the kindly, comical, nineteenth-century manner of Jo's German husband in *Little Men*, or in the manner of the crusading *sturm und drang* liberal scholars in second year German novels. "Eric's mother and father are *both* called Dr. Burckhard," my mother once said, and indeed there was something endearingly repellent about Mrs. Burckhard with her doctor's degree, her long, unstylish skirts, and her dramatic, dulling blond braids. Strangely the Burckhards' sober continental bourgeois house was without golden mean—everything was either hilariously old Swiss or madly modern. The Frau Doctor Burckhard used to serve mid-morning hot chocolate with rosettes of whipped cream, and receive her friends in a long, uncarpeted hall-drawing room with lethal ferns and a yellow beeswaxed hardwood floor shining under a central skylight. On the wall there were large expert photographs of what at a distance appeared to be Mont

Blanc—they were in reality views of Frank Lloyd Wright's Japanese hotel.

I admired the Burckhards and felt at home in their house, and these feelings were only intensified when I discovered that my mother was always ill at ease with them. The heartiness, the enlightenment, and the bright, ferny greenhouse atmosphere were too much for her.

Eric and I were too young to care for books or athletics. Neither of our houses had absorbing toys or an elevator to go up and down in. We were inseparable, but I cannot imagine what we talked about. I loved Eric because he was more popular than I and yet absolutely *sui generis* at the Brimmer School. He had a chalk-white face and limp, fine, white-blond hair. He was frail, elbowy, started talking with an enthusiastic Mont Blanc chirp and would flush with bewilderment if interrupted. All the other boys at Brimmer wore little tweed golf suits with knickerbockers, but Eric always arrived in a black suit coat, a Byronic collar, and cuff-less gray flannel trousers that almost hid his shoes. The long trousers were replaced on warm days by gray flannel shorts, such as were worn by children still in kindergarten. Eric's unenviable and freakish costumes were too old or too young. He accepted the whims of his parents with a buoyant tranquillity that I found unnatural.

My first and terminating quarrel with Eric was my fault. Eventually almost our whole class at Brimmer had whooping cough, but Eric's seizure was like his long trousers—untimely: he was sick a month too early. For a whole month he was in quarantine and forced to play by himself in a removed corner of the Public Garden. He was certainly conspicuous as he skiproped with his Swiss nurse under the out-of-the-way Ether Memorial Fountain far from the pond and the swan boats. His parents had decided that this was an excellent opportunity for Eric to brush up on his German, and so the absoluteness of his quarantine was monstrously exaggerated by the fact that child and nurse spoke no English but only a guttural, British-sounding, Swiss German. Round and round and round the

Fountain, he played intensely, frailly, obediently, until I began to tease him. Though motioned away by him, I came close. I had attracted some of the most popular Brimmer School boys. For the first time I had gotten favorable attention from several little girls. I came close. I shouted. Was Eric afraid of girls? I imitated his German. *Ein, swei, drei, BEER.* I imitated Eric's coughing. "He is afraid he will give you whooping cough if he talks or lets you come nearer," the nurse said in her musical Swiss-English voice. I came nearer. Eric flushed, grew white, bent double with coughing. He began to cry, and had to be led away from the Public Garden. For a whole week I routed Eric from the Garden daily, and for two or three days I was a center of interest. "Come see the Lake Geneva spider monkey!" I would shout. I don't know why I couldn't stop. Eric never told his father, I think, but when he recovered we no longer spoke. The breach was so unspoken and intense that our classmates were actually horrified. They even devised a solemn ritual for our reconciliation. We crossed our hearts, mixed spit, mixed blood. The reconciliation was hollow.

My parents' confidences and quarrels stopped each night at ten or eleven o'clock, when my father would hang up his tuxedo, put on his commander's uniform, and take a trolley back to the naval yard at Charlestown. He had just broken in a new car. Like a chauffeur, he watched this car, a Hudson, with an informed vigilance, always giving its engine hair-trigger little tinkerings of adjustment or friendship, always fearful lest the black body, unbeautiful as his boiled shirts, should lose its outline and gloss. He drove with flawless, almost instrumental, monotony. Mother, nevertheless, was forever encouraging him to walk or take taxis. She would tell him that his legs were growing vestigial from disuse and remind him of the time a jack had slipped and he had broken his leg while shifting a tire. "Alone and at night," she would say, "an amateur driver is unsafe in a car." Father sighed and obeyed—only, putting on a martyred and penny-saving face, he would keep his self-respect by taking the trolley rather than a taxi. Each night he shifted back into his uniform, but his departures from Revere Street were so furtive that several months passed before I realized what was happening—we had *two* houses! Our second house was the residence in the Naval Yard assigned to the third in command. It was large, had its own flagpole, and screen porches on three levels—yet it was something to be ashamed of. Whatever pomp or distinction its possession might have had for us was destroyed by an eccentric humiliation inflicted on Father by his superior, Admiral De Stahl, the commandant at Charlestown. De Stahl had not been consulted about our buying the 91 Revere Street house. He was outraged, stormed about "flaunting private fortunes in the face of naval tradition," and ordered my father to sleep on bounds at the Yard in the house provided for that purpose.

On our first Revere Street Christmas Eve, the telephone rang in the middle of dinner; it was Admiral De Stahl demanding Father's instant return to the Navy Yard. Soon Father was back in his uniform. In taking leave of my mother and grandparents he was, as was usual with him under pressure, a little evasive and magniloquent. "A woman works from sun to sun," he said, "but a sailor's watch is never done." He compared a naval officer's hours with a doctor's, hinted at surprise maneuvers, and explained away the uncommunicative arrogance of Admiral De Stahl: "The Old Man has to be hush-hush." Later that night, I lay in bed and tried to imagine that my father was leading his engineering force on a surprise maneuver through arctic wastes. A forlorn hope! "Hush-hush, hush-hush," whispered the snowflakes as big as street lamps as they broke on Father—broke and buried. Outside, I heard real people singing carols, shuffling snow off their shoes, opening and shutting doors. I worried at the meaning of a sentence I had heard quoted from the *Boston Evening Transcript*: "On this Christmas Eve, as usual, the whole of Beacon Hill can be expected to become a single old-fashioned open house—the names of mine host the Hill, and her guests will read like the contents of the Social

Register." I imagined Beacon Hill changed to the snow queen's palace, as vast as the north pole. My father pressed a cold finger to his lip: "hush-hush," and led his surprise squad of sailors around an altar, but the altar was a tremendous cash register, whose roughened nickel surface was cheaply decorated with trowels, pyramids, and Arabic swirls. A great drawer helplessly chopped back and forth, unable to shut because choked with greenbacks. "Hush-hush!" My father's engineers wound about me with their eye-patches, orange sashes, and curtain-ring earrings, like the Gilbert and Sullivan pirates' chorus. . . . Outside on the streets of Beacon Hill, it was night, it was dismal, it was raining. Something disturbing had befallen the familiar and honorable Salvation Army band; its big drum and accordion were now accompanied by drunken voices howling: *The Old Gray Mare, she ain't what she used to be, when Mary went to milk the cow.* A sound of a bosun's whistle. Women laughing. Someone repeatedly rang our doorbell. I heard my mother talking on the telephone. "Your inebriated sailors have littered my doorstep with the dregs of Scollay Square." There was a gloating panic in her voice that showed she enjoyed the drama of talking to Admiral De Stahl. "Sir," she shrilled, "you have compelled my husband to leave me alone and defenseless on Christmas Eve!" She ran into my bedroom. She hugged me. She said, "Oh Bobby, it's such a comfort to have a man in the house." "I am not a man," I said, "I am a boy."

Boy—at that time this word had private associations for me; it meant weakness, outlawry, and yet was a status to be held onto. Boys were a sideline at my Brimmer School. The eight superior grades were limited to girls. In these grades, moreover, scholarship was made subservient to discipline, as if in contempt of the male's two idols: career and earning power. The school's tone, its *ton*, was a blend of the feminine and the military, a bulky reality governed in turn by stridency, smartness, and steadiness. The girls wore white jumpers, black skirts, stockings, and rectangular low-heeled shoes. An ex-West Pointer had been appointed to teach drill; and, at the moment of my enrollment in Brimmer, our principal, the hitherto staid Miss Manice, was rumored to be showing signs of age and of undermining her position with the school trustees by girlish, quite out of character, rhapsodies on the varsity basketball team, winner of two consecutive championships. The lower four grades, peaceful and lackadaisical, were, on the other hand, almost a separate establishment. Miss Manice regarded these "coeducated" classes with amused carelessness, allowed them to wear their ordinary clothes, and . . . carelessness, however, is incorrect—Miss Manice, in her administration of the lower school, showed the inconsistency and euphoria of a dual personality. Here she mysteriously shed all her Prussianism. She quoted Emerson and Mencken, disparaged the English, threatened to break with the past, and boldly coquetted with the non-military American genius by displaying movies illustrating the careers of Edison and Ford. Favored lower school teachers were permitted to use us as guinea pigs for mildly radical experiments. At Brimmer I *un*learned writing. The script that I had mastered with much agony at my first school was denounced as illegible: I was taught to print according to the Dalton Plan—to this day, as a result, I have to print even my two middle names and can only really *write* two words: "Robert" and "Lowell." Our instruction was subject to bewildering leaps. The usual fall performance by the Venetian glass-blowers was followed by a tour of the Riverside Press. We heard Rudy Vallee, then heard spirituals sung by the Hampton Institute choir. We studied grammar from a formidable, unreconstructed textbook written by Miss Manice's father. There, I battled with figures of speech and Greek terminology: *Chiásmus*, the arrangement of corresponding words in opposite order; *Brachylogy*, the failure to repeat an element that is supplied in more or less modified form. Then all this pedantry was nullified by the introduction of a new textbook which proposed to lift the face of syntax by using game techniques and drawings.

Physical instruction in the lower school was irregular, spontaneous, and had nothing of that swept and garnished barrack-room cameraderie of the older girls' gymnasium exercises. On the roof of our school building, there was an ugly concrete area that looked as if it had been intended for the top floor of a garage. Here we played tag, drew lines with chalk, and chose up sides for a kind of kids' soccer. On bright spring days, Mr. Newell, a submerged young man from Boston University, took us on botanical hikes through the Arboretum. He had an eye for inessentials—read us Martha Washington's poems at the Old State House, pointed out the roof of Brimmer School from the top of the Customs House, made us count the steps of the Bunker Hill Monument, and one rainy afternoon broke all rules by herding us into the South Boston Aquarium in order to give an unhealthy, eager, little lecture on the sewage-consumption of the conger eel. At last Miss Manice seemed to have gotten wind of Mr. Newell's moods. For an afternoon or two she herself served as his substitute. We were walked briskly past the houses of Parkman and Dana, and assigned themes on the spunk of great persons who had overcome physical handicaps and risen to the top of the ladder. She talked about Elizabeth Barrett, Helen Keller; her pet theory, however, was that "women simply are not the equals of men." I can hear Miss Manice browbeating my white and sheepish father, "How can we stand up to you? Where are our Archimedeses, our Wagners, our Admiral Simses?" Miss Manice adored "Sir Walter Scott's *big bow-wow*," wished "Boston had banned the tubercular novels of the Brontës," and found nothing in the world "so simpatico" as the "strenuous life" lived by President Roosevelt. Yet the extravagant hysteria of Miss Manice's philanthropy meant nothing; Brimmer was entirely a woman's world—*dumkopf*, perhaps, but not in the least Quixotic, Brimmer was ruled by a woman's obvious aims and by her naive pragmatism. The quality of this regime, an extension of my mother's, shone out in full glory at general assemblies or when I sat with a handful of other boys on the bleachers of Brimmer's new Manice Hall. In unison our big girls sang "America"; back and forth our amazons tramped—their brows were wooden, their dress was black and white, and their columns followed standard-bearers holding up an American flag, the white flag of the Commonwealth of Massachusetts, and the green flag of Brimmer. At basketball games against Miss Lee's or Miss Winsor's, it was our upper-school champions who rushed onto the floor, as feline and fateful in their pace as lions. This was our own immediate and daily spectacle; in comparison such masculine displays as trips to battle cruisers commanded by comrades of my father seemed eyewash—the Navy moved in a realm as ghostlike and removed from my life as the elfin acrobatics of Douglas Fairbanks or Peter Pan. I wished I were an older girl. I wrote Santa Claus for a field hockey stick. To be a boy at Brimmer was to be small, denied, and weak.

I was promised an improved future and taken on Sunday afternoon drives through the suburbs to inspect the boys' schools: Rivers, Dexter, Country Day. These expeditions were stratagems designed to give me a chance to know my father; Mother noisily stayed behind and amazed me by pretending that I had forbidden her to embark on "men's work." Father, however, seldom insisted, as he should have, on seeing the headmasters in person, yet he made an astonishing number of friends; his trust begat trust, and something about his silences encouraged junior masters and even school janitors to pour out small talk that was detrimental to rival institutions. At each new school, however, all this gossip was easily refuted; worse still Mother was always ready to cross-examine Father in a manner that showed that she was asking questions for the purpose of giving, not of receiving, instruction; she expressed astonishment that a wishy-washy desire to be everything to everybody had robbed a naval man of any reliable concern for his son's welfare. Mother regarded the suburban schools as "gerrymandered" and middle-class; after Father had completed his round of inspections, she made her own follow-up visits and told Mr. Dexter and Mr. Rivers to their faces that she was looking for a "respectable stop-gap" for her son's "three years between Brimmer and Saint Mark's." Saint Mark's was the boarding school for which I had been enrolled at birth, and was due to enter in 1930. I distrusted change, knew each school since kindergarten had been more constraining and punitive than its predecessor, and believed the suburban country day schools were flimsily disguised fronts for reformatories. With the egotistic, slightly paranoid apprehensions of an only child, I wondered what became of boys graduating from Brimmer's fourth grade, feared the worst—we were darkly imperiled, like some annual bevy of Athenian youths destined for the Minotaur. And to judge from my father, men between the ages of six and sixty did nothing but meet new challenges, take on heavier responsibilities, and lose all freedom to explode. A ray of hope in the far future was my white-haired Grandfather Winslow, whose unchecked commands and demands were always upsetting people for their own good—he was all I could ever want to be: the bad boy, the problem child, the commodore of his household.

When I entered Brimmer I was eight and a half. I was distracted in my studies, assented to whatever I was told, picked my nose whenever no one was watching, and worried our third-grade teacher by organizing creepy little gangs of boys at recess. I was girl-shy. Thick-witted, narcissistic, thuggish, I had the conventional prepuberty character of my age; whenever a girl came near me, my whole person cringed like a sponge wrung dry by a clenching fist. I was less rather than more bookish than most children, but the girl I dreamed about continually had wheel-spoke black and gold eyelashes, double-length page-boy blond hair, a little apron, a bold, blunt face, a saucy, shivery way of talking, and . . . a paper body—she was the girl in John Tenniel's illustrations to *Alice in Wonderland*. The invigorating and symmetrical aplomb of my ideal Alice was soon enriched and nullified by a second face, when my father took me to the movies on the afternoon of one of Mother's headaches. An innocuous child's movie, the bloody, all-male *Beau Geste* had been chosen, but instead my father preferred a nostalgic tour of places he had enjoyed on shore leave. We went to the Majestic Theater where he had first seen Pola Negri—where we too saw Pola Negri, sloppy-haired, slack, yawning, ravaged, unwashed . . . an Anti-Alice.

Our class belles, the Norton twins, Elie and Lindy, fell far short of the Nordic Alice and the foreign Pola. Their prettiness, rather fluffy, freckled, bashful, might have escaped notice if they had been one instead of two, and if their manners had been less goodhumored, entertaining, and reliable. What mattered more than sex, athletics, or studies to us at Brimmer was our popularity; each child had an unwritten class-popularity poll inside his head. Everyone was ranked, and all day each of us mooned profoundly on his place, as it quivered like our blood or a compass needle with a thousand revisions. At nine character is, perhaps, too much *in ovo* for a child to be strongly disliked, but sitting next to Elie Norton, I glanced at her and gulped prestige from her popularity. We were not close at first; then nearness made us closer friends, for Elie had a gracious gift, the gift of gifts, I suppose, in a child: she forgot all about the popularity-rank of the classmate she was talking to. No moron could have seemed so uncritical as this airy, chatty, intelligent child, the belle of our grade. She noticed my habit of cocking my head on one side, shutting my eyes, and driving like a bull through opposition at soccer—wishing to amuse without wounding, she called me Buffalo Bull. At general assembly she would giggle with contented admiration at the upper-school girls in their penal black and white. "What bruisers, what beef-eaters! Dear girls," she would sigh, parroting her sophisticated mother, "we shall all become fodder for the governess classes before graduating from Brimmer." I felt that Elie Norton understood me better than anyone except my playful little Grandmother Winslow.

One morning there was a disaster. The boy behind me, no friend, had been tapping at my elbow for over a minute to catch my attention before I consented to look up and see a great golden puddle spreading toward me from under Elie's chair. I dared not speak, smile, or flicker an eyelash in her direction. She ran bawling from the classroom. Trying to catch every eye, yet avoid commitment, I gave sidelong and involuntary smirks at space. I began to feel manic with superiority to Elie Norton and struggled to swallow down a feeling of goaded hollowness—was I deserting her? Our teacher left us on our honor and ran down the hall. The class milled about in a hesitant hush. The girls blushed. The boys smirked. Miss Manice, the principal, appeared. She wore her whitish-brown dress with darker brown spots. Shimmering in the sunlight and chilling us, she stood mothlike in the middle of the classroom. We rushed to our seats. Miss Manice talked about how there was "nothing laughable about a malaise." She broke off. Her face took on an expression of invidious disgust. She was staring at me. . . . In the absentmindedness of my guilt and excitement, I had taken the nearest chair, the chair that Elie Norton had just left. "Lowell," Miss Manice shrieked, "are you going to soak there all morning like a bump on a log?"

When Elie Norton came back, there was really no break in her friendliness toward me, but there was something caved in, something crippled in the way I stood up to her and tried to answer her disengaged chatter. I thought about her all the time; seldom meeting her eyes now, I felt rich and raw in her nearness. I wanted passionately to stay on at Brimmer, and told my mother a fib one afternoon late in May of my last year. "Miss Manice has begged me to stay on," I said, "and enter the fifth grade." Mother pointed out that there had never been a boy in the fifth grade. Contradicted, I grew excited. "If Miss Manice has begged me to stay," I said, "why can't I stay?" My voice rose, I beat on the floor with my open hands. Bored and bewildered, my mother went upstairs with a headache. "If you won't believe me," I shouted after her, "why don't you telephone Miss Manice or Mrs. Norton?"

Brimmer School was thrown open on sunny March and April afternoons and our teachers took us for strolls on the polite, landscaped walks of the Public Garden. There I'd loiter by the old iron fence and gape longingly across Charles Street at the historic

Boston Common, a now largely wrong-side-of-the-tracks park. On the Common there were mossy bronze reliefs of Union soldiers, and a captured German tank filled with smelly wads of newspaper. Everywhere there were grit, litter, gangs of Irish, Negroes, Latins. On Sunday afternoons orators harangued about Sacco and Vanzetti, while others stood about heckling and blocking the sidewalks. Keen young policemen, looking for trouble, lolled on the benches. At nightfall a police lieutenant on horseback inspected the Common. In the Garden, however, there was only Officer Lever, a single white-haired and mustached dignitary, who had once been the doorman at the Union Club. He now looked more like a member of the club. "Lever's a man about town," my Grandfather Winslow would say. "Give him Harris tweeds and a glass of Scotch, and I'd take him for Cousin Herbert." Officer Lever was without thoughts or deeds, but Back Bay and Beacon Hill parents loved him just for being. No one asked this hollow and leonine King Log to be clairvoyant about children.

One day when the saucer magnolias were in bloom, I bloodied Bulldog Binney's nose against the pedestal of George Washington's statue in full view of Commonwealth Avenue; then I bloodied Dopey Dan Parker's nose; then I stood in the center of a sundial tulip bed and pelted a little enemy ring of third-graders with wet fertilizer. Officer Lever was telephoned. Officer Lever telephoned my mother. In the presence of my mother and some thirty nurses and children, I was expelled from the Public Garden. I was such a bad boy, I was told, "that *even* Officer Lever had been forced to put his foot down."

New England winters are long. Sunday mornings are long. Ours were often made tedious by preparations for dinner guests. Mother would start airing at nine. Whenever the air grew so cold that it hurt, she closed the den windows; then we were attacked by sour kitchen odors winding up a clumsily rebuilt dumb-waiter shaft. The windows were again thrown open. We sat in an atmosphere of glacial purity and sacrifice. Our breath puffed whitely. Father and I wore sleeveless cashmere jerseys Mother had bought at Filene's Basement. A do-it-yourself book containing diagrams for the correct carving of roasts lay on the arm of Father's chair. At hand were Big Bill Tilden on tennis, Capablanca on chess, newspaper clippings from Sidney Lenz's bridge column, and a magnificent tome with photographs and some American's nationalist sketch of Sir Thomas Lipton's errors in the Cup Defender races. Father made little progress in these diversions, and yet one of the authors assured him that mastery demanded only willing readers who understood the meaning of English words. Throughout the winter a gray-whiteness glared through the single den window. In the apoplectic brick alley, a fire escape stood out against our sooty plank fence. Father believed that churchgoing was undignified for a naval man; his Sunday mornings were given to useful acts such as lettering his three new galvanized garbage cans: R.T.S. LOWELL—U.S.N.

Our Sunday dinner guests were often naval officers. Naval officers were not Mother's sort; very few people *were* her sort in those days, and that was her trouble—a very authentic, human, and plausible difficulty, which made Mother's life one of much suffering. She did not have the self-assurance for wide human experience; she needed to feel liked, admired, surrounded by the approved and familiar. Her haughtiness and chilliness came from apprehension. She would start talking like a *grande dame* and then stand back rigid and faltering, as if she feared being crushed by her own massively intimidating offensive.

Father's old Annapolis roommate, Commander Billy "Battleship Bilge" Harkness, was a frequent guest at Revere Street and one that always threw Mother off balance. Billy was a rough diamond. He made jokes about his "all-American family tree," and insisted that his name, pronounced H*a*rkness, should be spelled H*e*rkness. He came from Louisville, Kentucky, drank whisky to "renew his Bourbon blood," and still spoke with an accent that sounded—so his colleagues said—"like a bran-fed stallion." Like my father, however, Commander Billy had entered the Naval Academy when he was a boy of fourteen; his Southernisms had been thoroughly rubbed away. He was teased for knowing nothing about race horses, mountaineers, folk ballads, hams, sour mash, tobacco . . . Kentucky Colonels. Though hardly an officer and a gentleman in the old Virginian style, he was an unusual combination of clashing virtues: he had led his class in the sciences and yet was what his superiors called "a *mathmaddition* with the habit of command." He and my father, the youngest men in their class, had often been shipmates. Bilge's executive genius had given color and direction to Father's submissive tenacity. He drank like a fish at parties, but was a total abstainer on duty. With reason Commander Harkness had been voted the man most likely to make a four-star admiral in the class of '07.

Billy called his wife *Jimmy* or *Jeems*, and had a rough friendly way of saying, "Oh, Jimmy's bright as a penny." Mrs. Harkness was an unpleasant rarity: she was the only naval officer's wife we knew who was also a college graduate. She had a flat flapper's figure, and hid her intelligence behind a nervous twitter of vulgarity and toadyism. "Charlotte," she would almost scream at Mother, "is this mirAGE, this MIRacle your *own* dining room!"

Then Mother might smile and answer in a distant, though cosy and amused, voice, "I usually manage to make myself pretty comfortable."

Mother's comfort was chic, romantic, impulsive. If her silver service shone, it shone with hectic perfection to rebuke the functional domesticity of naval wives. She had determined to make her *ambiance* beautiful and luxurious, but wanted neither her beauty nor her luxury unaccompanied. Beauty pursued too exclusively meant artistic fatuity of a kind made farcical by her Aunt Sarah Stark Winslow, a beauty too lofty and original ever to marry, a prima donna on the piano, too high-strung ever to give a public recital. Beauty alone meant the maudlin ignominy of having one's investments managed by interfering relatives. Luxury alone, on the other hand, meant for Mother the "paste and fool's-gold polish" that one met with in the foyer of the new Statler Hotel. She loathed the "undernourishment" of Professor Burckhard's Bauhaus modernism, yet in moments of pique she denounced our pompous Myers mahoganies as "suitable for politicians at the Bellevue Hotel." She kept a middle-of-the-road position, and much admired Italian pottery with its fresh peasant colors and puritanical, clean-cut lines. She was fond of saying, "The French *do* have taste," but spoke with a double-edged irony which implied the French, with no moral standards to support their finish, were really no better than naval yahoos. Mother's beautiful house was dignified by a rich veneer of the useful.

"I have always believed carving to be *the* gentlemanly talent," mother used to proclaim. Father, faced with this opinion, pored over his book of instructions or read the section on table carving in the Encyclopædia Britannica. Eventually he discovered among the innumerable small, specialized Boston "colleges" an establishment known as a carving school. Each Sunday from then on he would sit silent and erudite before his roast. He blinked, grew white, looked winded, and wiped beads of perspiration from his eyebrows. His purpose was to reproduce stroke by stroke his last carving lesson, and he worked with all the formal rightness and particular error of some shaky experiment in remote control. He enjoyed quiet witticisms at the expense of his carving master—"a philosopher who gave himself all the airs of a Mahan!" He liked to pretend that the carving master had stated that "No two cuts are identical," *ergo*: "each offers original problems for the *executioner*." Guests were appeased by Father's saying, "I am just a plebe at this guillotine. Have a hunk of my roast beef hash."

What angered Father was Mrs. Harkness's voice grown merciless with excitement, as she studied his hewing and hacking. She was sure to say something tactless about how Commander Billy was "a stingy artist at carving who could shave General Washington off the dollar bill."

Nothing could stop Commander Billy, that born carver, from reciting verses:

> *"By carving my way*
> *I lived on my pay;*
> *This reeward, though small,*
> *Beats none at all . . .*
>
> *My carving paper-thin*
> *Can make a guinea hin,*
> *All giblets, bones, and skin,*
> *Canteen a party of tin."*

And I, furious for no immediate reason, blurted out, "Mother, how much does Grandfather Winslow have to fork up to pay for Daddy's carving school?"

These Sunday dinners with the Harknesses were always woundingly boisterous affairs. Father, unnaturally outgoing, would lead me forward and say, "Bilge, I want you to meet my first coupon from the bond of matrimony."

Commander Billy would answer, "So this is the range-finder you are raising for future wars!" They would make me salute, stand at attention, stand at ease. "Angel-face," Billy would say to me, "you'll skipper a flivver."

"Jimmy" Harkness, of course, knew that Father was anxiously negotiating with Lever Brothers' Soap, and arranging for his resignation from the service, but nothing could prevent her from proposing time and again her "hens' toast to the drakes." Dragging Mother to her feet, Jimmy would scream, "To Bob and Bilgy's next battleship together!"

What Father and Commander Billy enjoyed talking about most was their class of '07. After dinner, the ladies would retire to the upstairs sitting room. As a special privilege I was allowed to remain at the table with the men. Over and over, they would talk about their ensigns' cruise around the world, escaping the "reeport," gunboating on the upper Yangtze during the Chinese Civil War, keeping sane and sanitary at Guantanamo, patroling the Golfo del Papayo during the two-bit Nicaraguan Revolution, when water to wash in cost a dollar a barrel and was mostly "alkali and wrigglers." There were the class casualties: Holden and Holcomb drowned in a foundered launch off Hampton Roads; "Count" Bowditch, killed by the Moros and famous for his dying words to Commander Harkness: "I'm all right. Get on the job, Bilge."

They would speak about the terrible 1918 influenza epidemic, which had killed more of their classmates than all the skirmishes or even the World War. It was an honor, however, to belong to a class which included "Chips" Carpender, whose destroyer, the *Fanning*, was the only British or American warship to force a German submarine to break water and surrender. It was a feather in their caps that three of their classmates, Bellinger, Reade, and another, should have made the first trans-Atlantic seaplane flight. They put their faith in teamwork, and Lindbergh's solo hop to Paris struck them as unprofessional, a newspaper trick. What made Father and Commander Billy mad as hornets was the mare's-nest made of naval administration by "deserving Democrats." Hadn't Secretary of State Bryan ordered their old battlewagon the *Idaho* to sail on a goodwill mission to Switzerland? "Bryan, Bryan, Bryan," Commander Billy would boom, "the pious swab had been told that Lake Geneva had annexed the Adriatic." Another "guy with false gills," Josephus Daniels, "ordained by Divine Providence Secretary of the Navy," had refused to send Father and Billy to the war zone. "You are looking," Billy would declaim, "at martyrs in the famous victory of red tape. Our names are rubric." A man they had to take their hats off to was Theodore Roosevelt; Billy had been one of the lucky ensigns who had helped "escort the redoubtable Teddy to Panama." Perhaps because of his viciously inappropriate nickname, "Bilge,"

Commander Harkness always spoke with brutal facetiousness against the class *bilgers*, officers whose "services were no longer required by the service." In more Epicurean moods, Bilge would announce that he "meant to accumulate a lot of dough from complacent, well-meaning, although misguided West Point officers gullible enough to bet their shirts on the Army football team."

"Let's have a squint at your *figger* and waterline, Bob," Billy would say. He'd admire Father's trim girth and smile familiarly at his bald spot. "Bob," he'd say, "you've maintained your displacement and silhouette unmodified, except for somewhat thinner top chafing gear."

Commander Billy's drinking was a "pain in the neck." He would take possession of Father's sacred "rhino" armchair, sprawl legs astraddle, make the tried and true framework groan, and crucify Mother by roaring out verbose toasts in what he called "me boozy cockney-h'Irish." He would drink to our cocktail shaker. " 'Ere's to the 'older of the Lowelldom nectar," he would bellow. "Hip, hip, hooray for senor Martino, h'our h'old hipmate, 'elpmate, and hhonorary member of '07—h'always h'able to navigate and never says dry." We never got through a visit without one of Billy's "Bottoms up to the 'ead of the Nation. 'Ere's to herb-garden 'Erb." This was a swaggering dig at Herbert Hoover's notoriously correct, but insular, refusal to "imbibe anything more potent than Bromo-Seltzer" at a war-relief banquet in Brussels. Commander Billy's bulbous, water-on-the-brain forehead would glow and trickle with fury. Thinking on Herbert Hoover and Prohibition, he was unable to contain himself. "What a hick! We haven't been steered by a gentleman of parts since the redoubtable Teddy." He recited *wet* verses, such as the following inserted in Father's class book:

"I tread the bridge with measured pace;
Proud, yet anguish marks my face—
What worries me like crushing sin
Is where on the sea can I buy dry gin?"

In his cups, Commander Bilge acted as though he owned us. He looked like a human ash-heap. Cigar ashes buried the heraldic hedgehog on the ash tray beside him; cigar ashes spilled over and tarnished the golden stork embroidered on the table-cover; cigar ashes littered his own shiny blue-black uniform. Greedily Mother's eyes would brighten, drop and brighten. She would say darkly, "I was brought up by Papá to be like a naval officer, to be ruthlessly neat."

Once Commander Billy sprawled back so recklessly that the armchair began to come apart. "You see, Charlotte," he said to Mother, "at the height of my *climacteric* I am breaking Bob's chair."

Harkness went in for tiresome, tasteless harangues against Amy Lowell, which he seemed to believe necessary for the enjoyment of his after-dinner cigar. He would point a stinking baby stogie at Mother. " 'Ave a peteeto cigareeto, Charlotte," he would crow. "Puff on this whacking black cheroot, and you'll be a match for any reeking senorita *femme fatale* in the spiggotty republics, where blindness from Bob's bathtub hooch is still unknown. When you go up in smoke, Charlotte, remember the *Maine*. Remember Amy Lowell, that cigar-chawing, guffawing, senseless and meterless, multimillionheiress, heavyweight mascot on a floating fortress. Damn the *Patterns*! Full speed ahead on a cigareeto!"

Amy Lowell was never a welcome subject in our household. Of course, no one spoke disrespectfully of Miss Lowell. She had been so plucky, so *formidable, so beautifully and unblushingly immense*, as Henry James might have said. And yet, though irreproachably decent herself apparently, like Mae West she seemed to provoke indecorum in others. There was an anecdote which I was too young to understand: it was about Amy's getting her migraine headaches from being kept awake by the exercises of honeymooners in an adjacent New York hotel room. Amy's relatives would have liked to have honored her as a *personage*, a personage a little *outrée* perhaps, but perfectly within the natural order, like

Amy's girlhood idol, the Duse. Or at least she might have been unambiguously tragic, short-lived, and a classic, like her last idol, John Keats. My parents piously made out a case for Miss Lowell's *Life of Keats*, which had killed its author and was so much more manly and intelligible than her poetry. Her poetry! But was *poetry* what one could call Amy's loud, bossy, unladylike *chinoiserie*— her free verse! For those that could understand it, her matter was, no doubt, blameless, but the effrontery of her manner made my parents relish Robert Frost's remark that "writing free verse was like playing tennis without a net."

Whenever Amy Lowell was mentioned Mother bridled. Not distinguishing, not caring whether her relative were praised or criticized, she would say, "Amy had the courage of her convictions. She worked like a horse." Mother would conclude characteristically, "Amy did insist on doing everything the *hard* way. I think, perhaps, that her brother, the President of Harvard, did more for *other* people."

Often Father seemed to pay little attention to the conversation of his guests. He would smack his lips, and beam absentmindedly and sensuously, as if he were anticipating the comforts of civilian life—a perpetual shore leave in Hawaii. The Harknesses, however, cowed him. He would begin to feel out the subject of his resignation and observe in a wheedle obscurely loaded with significance that "certain *cits*, no brighter than you or I, pay income taxes as large as a captain's yearly salary."

Commander Harkness, unfortunately, was inclined to draw improper conclusions from such remarks. Disregarding the "romance of commerce," he would break out into ungentlemanly tirades against capital. "Yiss, old Bob," he would splutter, "when I consider the ungodly hoards garnered in by the insurance and broking gangs, it breaks my heart. Riches, reaches, overreaches! If Bob and I had half the swag that Harkness of Yale has just given Lowell of Harvard to build Georgian houses for Boston quee-eers with British accents!" He rumbled on morosely about retired naval officers "forced to live like coolies on their half-pay. Hurrah for the Bull Moose Party!" he'd shout. "Hurrah for Boss Curley! Hurrah for the Bolshies!"

Nothing prevented Commander Billy from telling about his diplomatic mission in 1918, when "his eyes had seen the Bolshie on his native heath." He had been in Budapest "during the brief sway of Béla Kun-Whon. Béla was giving those Hunkyland money-bags and educators the boot into the arms of American philanthropy!"

Then Mother would say, hopefully, "Mamá always said that the *old* Hungarians *did* have taste. Billy, your reference to Budapest makes me heartsick for Europe. I am dying for Bob and Bobby's permission to spend next summer at Etretat."

Commander Billy Harkness specialized in verses like "The Croix de Guerre":

> *"I toast the guy, who, crossing over,*
> *Abode in London for a year,*
> *The guy who to his wife and lover*
> *Returned with conscience clean and clear,*
> *Who nightly prowling Piccadilly*
> *Gave icy stares to floozies wild,*
> *And when approached said, 'Bilgy Billy*
> *Is mama's darling angel child—'*
> *Now he's the guy who rates the croy dee geer!"*

Mother, however, smiled mildly. "Billy," she would say, "my cousin, Admiral Ledyard Atkinson, always has a twinkle in his eye when he asks after your *vers de société*."

" 'Tommy' Atkins!" snorted Commander Billy. "I know Tommy better than my own mother. He's the first chapter in a book I'm secretly writing and leaving to the archives called *Wild Admirals I Have Known*. And now my bodily presence may no longer grace the inner sanctum of the Somerset Club, for fear Admiral Tommy'll assault me with five new chapters of his *Who Won the Battle of Jutland?*"

After the heat and push of Commander Billy, it was pleasant to sit in the shade of the Atkinsons. Cousin Ledyard wasn't exactly an admiral: he had been promoted to this rank during the World War and had soon reverted back to his old rank of captain. In 1926 he was approaching the retiring age and was still a captain. He was in charge of a big, stately, comfortable, but anomalous warship, which seldom sailed further than hailing distance from its Charlestown drydock. He was himself stately and anomalous. Serene, silver-maned, and Spanish-looking, Cousin Ledyard liked full-dress receptions and crowed like a rooster in his cabin crowded with liveried Filipinos, Cuban trophies, and racks of experimental firearms, such as pepper-box pistols and a machine gun worked by electric batteries. He rattled off Spanish phrases, told first-hand adventure stories about service with Admiral Schley, and reminded one of some landsman and diplomat commanding a galleon in Philip II's Armada. With his wife's money he had bought a motor launch which had a teak deck and a newfangled diesel engine. While his warship perpetually rode at anchor, Cousin Ledyard was forever hurrying about the harbor in his launch. "Oh, Led Atkinson has dash and his own speedboat!" This was about the best my father could bring himself to say for his relative. Commander Billy, himself a man of action, was more sympathetic: "Tommy's about a hundred horse and buggy power." Such a dinosaur, however, had little to offer an '07 Annapolis graduate. Billy's final judgment was that Cousin Ledyard knew less *trig* than a schoolgirl, had been promoted through mistaken identity or merely as "window-dressing," and "was really plotting to put airplane carriers in square sails to stem the tide of our declining Yankee seamanship." Mother lost her enthusiasm for Captain Atkinson's stately chatter—he was "unable to tell one woman from another."

Cousin Ledyard's wife, a Schenectady Hoes distantly related to my still living Great-Grandmother Myers, was twenty years younger than her husband. This made her a trying companion; with the energy of youth she demanded the homage due to age.

Once while playing in the Mattapoisett tennis tournament, she had said to her opponent, a woman her own age but married to a young husband, "I believe I'll call you Ruth; you can call me Mrs. Atkinson." She was a radiant Christian Scientist, darted about in smart serge suits and blouses frothing with lace. She filled her purse with Science literature and boasted without irony of "Boston's greatest grand organ" in the Christian Science mother temple on Huntington Avenue. As a girl, she had grown up with our Myers furniture. We dreaded Mrs. Atkinson's descents on Revere Street. She pooh-poohed Mother's taste, snorted at our ignorance of Myers family history, treated us as mere custodians of the Myers furniture, resented alterations, and had the memory of a mastodon for Cousin Cassie's associations with each piece. She wouldn't hear of my mother's distress from neuralgia, dismissed my asthma as "growing-pains," and sought to rally us by gossiping about healers. She talked a prim, sprightly babble. Like many Christian Scientists, she had a bloodless, euphoric, inexhaustible interest in her own body. In a discourse which lasted from her first helping of roast beef through her second demitasse, Mrs. Atkinson held us spellbound by telling how her healer had "surprised and evaporated a cyst inside a sac" inside her "major intestine."

I can hear my father trying to explain his resignation from the Navy to Cousin Ledyard or Commander Billy. Talking with an unnatural and importunate jocularity, he would say, "Billy Boy, it's a darned shame, but this State of Massachusetts doesn't approve of the service using its franchise and voting by mail. I haven't had a chance to establish residence since our graduation in '07. I think I'll put my blues in mothballs and become a *cit* just to prove I still belong to the country. The directors of Lever Brothers' Soap in Cambridge . . . I guess for *cits*, Billy, they've really got something on the ball, because they tell me they want me on their team."

Or Father, Cousin Ledyard, Commander Billy, and I would be

sitting on after dinner at the dining-room table and talking man to man. Father would say, "I'm afraid I'll grow dull and drab with all this goldbricking ashore. I am too old for tennis singles, but too young for that confirmed state of senility known as golf."

Cousin Ledyard and Commander Billy would puff silently on their cigars. Then Father would try again and say pitifully, "I don't think a naval man can ever on the *outside* replace the friends he made during his years of wearing the blue."

Then Cousin Ledyard would give Father a polite, funereal look and say, "Speaking of golf, Bob, you've hit me below the belt. I've been flubbing away at the game for thirty years without breaking ninety."

Commander Billy was blunter. He would chaff Father about becoming a "beachcomber" or "purser for the Republican junior chamber of commerce." He would pretend that Father was in danger of being jailed for evading taxes to support "Uncle Sam's circus." *Circus* was Commander Billy's slang for the Navy. The word reminded him of a comparison, and once he stood up from the table and bellowed solemnly: "Oyez, oyez! Bob Lowell, our bright boy, our class baby, is now on a par with 'Rattle-Ass Rats' Richardson, who resigned from us to become press agent for Sells-Floto Circus, and who writes me: 'Bilgy Dear—Beating the drum ahead of the elephants and the spangled folk, I often wonder why I run into so few of my classmates.' "

Those dinners, those apologies! Perhaps I exaggerate their embarassment because they hover so grayly in recollection and seem to anticipate ominously my father's downhill progress as a civilian and Bostonian. It was to be expected, I suppose, that Father should be in irons for a year or two, while becoming detached from his old comrades and interests, while waiting for the new life.

I used to sit through the Sunday dinners absorbing cold and anxiety from the table. I imagined myself hemmed in by our new, inherited Victorian Myers furniture. In the bleak Revere Street dining room, none of these pieces had at all that air of unhurried condescension that had been theirs behind the summery veils of tissue paper in Cousin Cassie Julian-James's memorial volume. Here, table, highboy, chairs, and screen—mahogany, cherry, teak—looked nervous and disproportioned. They seemed to wince, touch elbows, shift from foot to foot. High above the highboy, our gold National Eagle stooped forward, plastery and doddering. The Sheffield silver-plate urns, more precious than solid sterling, peeled; the bodies of the heraldic mermaids on the Mason-Myers crest blushed a metallic copper tan. In the harsh New England light, the bronze sphinxes supporting our sideboard looked as though manufactured in Grand Rapids. All too clearly no one had worried about synchronizing the grandfather clock's minutes, days, and months with its mellow old Dutch seascape-painted discs for showing the phases of the moon. The stricken, but still striking gong made sounds like steam banging through pipes. Colonel Myers' monumental Tibetan screen had been impiously shortened to fit it for a low Yankee ceiling. And now, rough and gawky, like some Hindu water buffalo killed in mid-rush but still alive with mad momentum, the screen hulked over us . . . and hid the pantry sink.

Our real blue-ribbon-winning *bête noire* was of course the portrait of Cousin Cassie's father, Mordecai Myers' fourth and most illustrious son: Colonel Theodorus Bailey Myers. The Colonel, like half of our new portraits, was merely a collateral relation; though really as close to us as James Russell Lowell, no one called the Colonel "Great Grand Uncle," and Mother playfully pretended that her mind was overstrained by having to remember his full name, rank, and connection. In the portrait, Colonel Theodorus wore a black coat and gray trousers, an obsequiously conservative costume which one associated with undertakers and the musicians at Symphony Hall. His spats were pearl gray plush with pearl buttons. His mustache might have been modeled on the mustache of a bartender in a Western. The majestic Tibetan screen enclosed him as though he were an ancestor-god from Lhasa, a blasphemous yet bogus attitude. Mr. Myers' colonel's tabs were crudely stitched to a civilian coat; his New York Yacht Club button glowed like a carnation; his vainglorious picture frame was a foot and a half wide. Forever, his right hand hovered over a glass dome that covered a model locomotive. He was vaguely Middle-Eastern and waiting. A lady in Mother's sewing circle had pertly interpreted this portrait as, "King Solomon about to receive the Queen of Sheba's shares in the Boston and Albany Railroad." Gone now was the Colonel's place of honor at Cousin Cassie's Washington mansion; gone was his charming satire on the belles of 1850, entitled, *Nothing to Wear*, which had once been quoted "throughout the length and breadth of the land as generally as was Bret Harte's *Heathen Chinee*"; gone was his priceless collection of autographed letters of *all* the Signers of the Declaration of Independence—he had said once, "my letters will be my tombstone." Colonel Theodorus Bailey Myers had never been a New Englander. His family tree reached to no obscure Somersetshire yeoman named Winslowe or Lowle. He had never even, like his father, Mordecai, gloried in a scarlet War of 1812 waistcoat. His portrait was an indifferent example from a dull, bad period. The Colonel's only son had sheepishly changed his name from Mason-Myers to Myers-Mason.

Waiting for dinner to end and for the guests to leave, I used to lean forward on my elbows, support each cheekbone with a thumb, and make my fingers meet in a clumsy Gothic arch across my forehead. I would stare through this arch and try to make life stop. Out in the alley the sun shone irreverently on our three garbage cans lettered: R.T.S. LOWELL—U.S.N. When I shut my eyes to stop the sun, I saw first an orange disc, then a red disc, then the portrait of Major Myers apotheosized, as it were, by the sunlight lighting the blood smear of his scarlet waistcoat. Still there was no *coup de théâtre* about the Major as he looked down on us with his portly young man's face of a comfortable upper New York State patroon and the friend of Robert Livingston and

Martin Van Buren. Great-great-Grandfather Myers had never frowned down in judgment on a Salem witch. There was no allegory in his eyes, no *Mayflower*. Instead he looked peacefully at his sideboard, his cut-glass decanters, his cellaret—the worldly bosom of the Mason-Myers mermaid engraved on a silver-plated urn. If he could have spoken, Mordecai would have said, "My children, my blood, accept graciously the loot of your inheritance. We are all dealers in used furniture."

The man who seems in my memory to sit under old Mordecai's portrait is not my father, but Commander Billy—*the* Commander after Father had thrown in his commission. There Billy would sit glowing, perspiring, bragging. Despite his rowdiness, he even then breathed the power that would make him a vice-admiral and hero in World War II. I can hear him boasting in lofty language of how he had stood up for democracy in the day of Lenin and Béla Kun; of how he "practiced the sport of kings" (i.e., commanded a destroyer) and combed the Mediterranean, Adriatic, and Black Seas like gypsies—seldom knowing what admiral he served under or where his next meal or load of fuel oil was coming from.

It always vexed the Commander, however, to think of the strings that had been pulled to have Father transferred from Washington to Boston. He would ask Mother, "Why in God's name should a man with Bob's brilliant cerebellum go and mess up his record by actually *begging* for that impotent field nigger's job of second in command at the defunct Boston Yard!"

I would squirm. I dared not look up because I knew that the Commander abhorred Mother's dominion over my father, thought my asthma, supposedly brought on by the miasmal damp of Washington, a myth, and considered our final flight to Boston a scandal.

My mother, on the other hand, would talk back sharply and explain to Billy that there was nothing second-string about the Boston Yard except its commandant, Admiral De Stahl, who had gone into a frenzy when he learned that my parents, supposed to live at the naval yard, had set themselves up without his permission at 91 Revere Street. The Admiral had *commanded* Father to reside at the yard, but Mother had bravely and stubbornly held on at Revere Street.

"A really great person," she would say, "knows how to be courteous to his superiors."

Then Commander Harkness would throw up his hands in despair and make a long buffoonish speech. "Would you believe it?" he'd say. "De Stahl, the anile slob, would make Bob Lowell sleep seven nights a week and twice on Sundays in that venerable twenty-room pile provided for his third in command at the yard. 'Bobby me boy,' the Man says, 'henceforth I will that you sleep wifeless. You're to push your beauteous mug into me boudoir each night at ten-thirty and each morn at six. And don't mind me laying to alongside the Missus De Stahl,' the old boy squeaks; 'we're just two oldsters as weak as babies. But Robbie Boy,' he says, 'don't let me hear of you hanging on your telephone wire and bending off the ear of that forsaken frau of yours sojourning on Revere Street. I might have to phone you in a hurry, if I should happen to have me stroke.' "

Taking hold of the table with both hands, the Commander tilted his chair backwards and gaped down at me with sorrowing Gargantuan wonder: "I know why Young Bob is an only child."

Part Three

Part Three

Ford Madox Ford

1873–1939

The lobbed ball plops, then dribbles to the cup. . . .
(a birdie Fordie!) But it nearly killed
the ministers. Lloyd George was holding up
the flag. He gabbled, "Hop-toad, hop-toad, hop-toad!
Hueffer has used a niblick on the green;
it's filthy art, Sir, filthy art!"
You answered, "What is art to me and thee?
Will a blacksmith teach a midwife how to bear?"
That cut the puffing statesman down to size,
Ford. You said, "Otherwise,
I would have been general of a division." Ah Ford!
Was it war, the sport of kings, that your *Good Soldier*,
the best French novel in the language, taught
those Georgian Whig magnificoes at Oxford,
at Oxford decimated on the Somme?
Ford, five times black-balled for promotion,
then mustard gassed voiceless some seven miles
behind the lines at Nancy or Belleau Wood:
you emerged in your "worn uniform,
gilt dragons on the revers of the tunic,"
a Jonah—O divorced, divorced
from the whale-fat of post-war London! Boomed,
cut, plucked and booted! In Provence, New York . . .
marrying, blowing . . . nearly dying
at Boulder, when the altitude
pressed the world on your heart,
and your audience, almost football-size,
shrank to a dozen, while you stood
mumbling, with fish-blue-eyes,
and mouth pushed out

fish-fashion, as if you gagged for air. . . .
Sandman! Your face, a childish *O*. The sun
is pernod-yellow and it gilds the heirs
of all the ages there on Washington
and Stuyvesant, your Lilliputian squares,
where writing turned your pockets inside out.
But master, mammoth mumbler, tell me why
the bales of your left-over novels buy
less than a bandage for your gouty foot.
Wheel-horse, *O* unforgetting elephant,
I hear you huffing at your old Brevoort,
Timon and Falstaff, while you heap the board
for publishers. Fiction! I'm selling short
your lies that made the great your equals. Ford,
you were a kind man and you died in want.

For George Santayana
1863–1952

In the heydays of 'forty-five,
bus-loads of souvenir-deranged
G.I.'s and officer-professors of philosophy
came crashing through your cell,
puzzled to find you still alive,
free-thinking Catholic infidel,
stray spirit, who'd found
the Church too good to be believed.
Later I used to dawdle
past Circus and Mithraic Temple
to *Santo Stefano* grown paper-thin
like you from waiting. . . .
There at the monastery hospital,
you wished those geese-girl sisters wouldn't bother
their heads and yours by praying for your soul:
"There is no God and Mary is His Mother."

Lying outside the consecrated ground
forever now, you smile
like Ser Brunetto running for the green
cloth at Verona—not like one
who loses, but like one who'd won . . .
as if your long pursuit of Socrates'
demon, man-slaying Alcibiades,
the demon of philosophy, at last had changed
those fleeting virgins into friendly laurel trees
at *Santo Stefano Rotondo*, when you died
near ninety,
still unbelieving, unconfessed and unreceived,
true to your boyish shyness of the Bride.

Old trooper, I see your child's red crayon pass,
bleeding deletions on the galleys you hold
under your throbbing magnifying glass,
that worn arena, where the whirling sand
and broken-hearted lions lick your hand
refined by bile as yellow as a lump of gold.

To Delmore Schwartz

(Cambridge 1946)

We couldn't even keep the furnace lit!
Even when we had disconnected it,
the antiquated
refrigerator gurgled mustard gas
through your mustard-yellow house,
and spoiled our long maneuvered visit
from T. S. Eliot's brother, Henry Ware. . . .

Your stuffed duck craned toward Harvard from my trunk:
its bill was a black whistle, and its brow
was high and thinner than a baby's thumb;
its webs were tough as toenails on its bough.
It was your first kill; you had rushed it home,
pickled in a tin wastebasket of rum—
it looked through us, as if it'd died dead drunk.
You must have propped its eyelids with a nail,
and yet it lived with us and met our stare,
Rabelaisian, lubricious, drugged. And there,
perched on my trunk and typing-table,
it cooled our universal
Angst a moment, Delmore. We drank and eyed
the chicken-hearted shadows of the world.
Underseas fellows, nobly mad,
we talked away our friends. "Let Joyce and Freud,
the Masters of Joy,
be our guests here," you said. The room was filled
with cigarette smoke circling the paranoid,
inert gaze of Coleridge, back
from Malta—his eyes lost in flesh, lips baked and black.
Your tiger kitten, *Oranges*,

cartwheeled for joy in a ball of snarls.
You said:
"We poets in our youth begin in sadness;
thereof in the end come despondency and madness;
Stalin has had two cerebral hemorrhages!"
The Charles
River was turning silver. In the ebb-
light of morning, we stuck
the duck
-'s web-
foot, like a candle, in a quart of gin we'd killed.

Words for Hart Crane

"When the Pulitzers showered on some dope
or screw who flushed our dry mouths out with soap,
few people would consider why I took
to stalking sailors, and scattered Uncle Sam's
phoney gold-plated laurels to the birds.
Because I knew my Whitman like a book,
stranger in America, tell my country: I,
Catullus redivivus, once the rage
of the Village and Paris, used to play my role
of homosexual, wolfing the stray lambs
who hungered by the Place de la Concorde.
My profit was a pocket with a hole.
Who asks for me, the Shelley of my age,
must lay his heart out for my bed and board."

Part Four

LIFE STUDIES

I

My Last Afternoon with Uncle Devereux Winslow

1922: the stone porch of my Grandfather's summer house

I.
"I won't go with you. I want to stay with Grandpa!"
That's how I threw cold water
on my Mother and Father's
watery martini pipe dreams at Sunday dinner.
. . . Fontainebleau, Mattapoisett, Puget Sound. . . .
Nowhere was anywhere after a summer
at my Grandfather's farm.
Diamond-pointed, athirst and Norman,
its alley of poplars
paraded from Grandmother's rose garden
to a scary stand of virgin pine,
scrub, and paths forever pioneering.

One afternoon in 1922,
I sat on the stone porch, looking through
screens as black-grained as drifting coal.
Tockytock, tockytock
clumped our Alpine, Edwardian cuckoo clock,
slung with strangled, wooden game.
Our farmer was cementing a root-house under the hill.
One of my hands was cool on a pile
of black earth, the other warm
on a pile of lime. All about me
were the works of my Grandfather's hands:
snapshots of his *Liberty Bell* silver mine;
his high school at *Stukkert am Neckar*;

stogie-brown beams; fools'-gold nuggets;
octagonal red tiles,
sweaty with a secret dank, crummy with ant-stale;
a Rocky Mountain chaise longue,
its legs, shellacked saplings.
A pastel-pale Huckleberry Finn
fished with a broom straw in a basin
hollowed out of a millstone.
Like my Grandfather, the décor
was manly, comfortable,
overbearing, disproportioned.

What were those sunflowers? Pumpkins floating shoulder-high?
It was sunset, Sadie and Nellie
bearing pitchers of ice-tea,
oranges, lemons, mint, and peppermints,
and the jug of shandygaff,
which Grandpa made by blending half and half
yeasty, wheezing homemade sarsaparilla with beer.
The farm, entitled *Char-de-sa*
in the Social Register,
was named for my Grandfather's children:
Charlotte, Devereux, and Sarah.
No one had died there in my lifetime . . .
Only Cinder, our Scottie puppy
paralyzed from gobbling toads.
I sat mixing black earth and lime.

II.
I was five and a half.
My formal pearl gray shorts
had been worn for three minutes.
My perfection was the Olympian
poise of my models in the imperishable autumn

display windows
of Rogers Peet's boys' store below the State House
in Boston. Distorting drops of water
pinpricked my face in the basin's mirror.
I was a stuffed toucan
with a bibulous, multicolored beak.

III.
Up in the air
by the lakeview window in the billiards-room,
lurid in the doldrums of the sunset hour,
my Great Aunt Sarah
was learning *Samson and Delilah*.
She thundered on the keyboard of her dummy piano,
with gauze curtains like a boudoir table,
accordionlike yet soundless.
It had been bought to spare the nerves
of my Grandmother,
tone-deaf, quick as a cricket,
now needing a fourth for "Auction,"
and casting a thirsty eye
on Aunt Sarah, risen like the phoenix
from her bed of troublesome snacks and Tauchnitz classics.

Forty years earlier,
twenty, auburn headed,
grasshopper notes of genius!
Family gossip says Aunt Sarah
tilted her archaic Athenian nose
and jilted an Astor.
Each morning she practiced
on the grand piano at Symphony Hall,
deathlike in the off-season summer—
its naked Greek statues draped with purple

like the saints in Holy Week. . . .
On the recital day, she failed to appear.

IV.
I picked with a clean finger nail at the blue anchor
on my sailor blouse washed white as a spinnaker.
What in the world was I wishing?
. . . A sail-colored horse browsing in the bulrushes . . .
A fluff of the west wind puffing
my blouse, kiting me over our seven chimneys,
troubling the waters. . . .
As small as sapphires were the ponds: *Quittacus, Snippituit,*
and *Assawompset,* halved by "the Island,"
where my Uncle's duck blind
floated in a barrage of smoke-clouds.
Double-barrelled shotguns
stuck out like bundles of baby crow-bars.
A single sculler in a camouflaged kayak
was quacking to the decoys. . . .

At the cabin between the waters,
the nearest windows were already boarded.
Uncle Devereux was closing camp for the winter.
As if posed for "the engagement photograph,"
he was wearing his severe
war-uniform of a volunteer Canadian officer.
Daylight from the doorway riddled his student posters,
tacked helter-skelter on walls as raw as a board-walk.
Mr. Punch, a water melon in hockey tights,
was tossing off a decanter of Scotch.
La Belle France in a red, white and blue toga
was accepting the arm of her "protector,"
the ingenu and porcine Edward VII.
The pre-war music hall belles

had goose necks, glorious signatures, beauty-moles,
and coils of hair like rooster tails.
The finest poster was two or three young men in khaki kilts
being bushwhacked on the veldt—
They were almost life-size. . . .

My Uncle was dying at twenty-nine.
"You are behaving like children,"
said my Grandfather,
when my Uncle and Aunt left their three baby daughters,
and sailed for Europe on a last honeymoon . . .
I cowered in terror.
I wasn't a child at all—
unseen and all-seeing, I was Agrippina
in the Golden House of Nero. . . .
Near me was the white measuring-door
my Grandfather had pencilled with my Uncle's heights.
In 1911, he had stopped growing at just six feet.
While I sat on the tiles,
and dug at the anchor on my sailor blouse,
Uncle Devereux stood behind me.
He was as brushed as Bayard, our riding horse.
His face was putty.
His blue coat and white trousers
grew sharper and straighter.
His coat was a blue jay's tail,
his trousers were solid cream from the top of the bottle.
He was animated, hierarchical,
like a ginger snap man in a clothes-press.
He was dying of the incurable Hodgkin's disease. . . .
My hands were warm, then cool, on the piles
of earth and lime,
a black pile and a white pile. . . .
Come winter,
Uncle Devereux would blend to the one color.

Dunbarton

My Grandfather found
his grandchild's fogbound solitudes
sweeter than human society.

When Uncle Devereux died,
Daddy was still on sea-duty in the Pacific;
it seemed spontaneous and proper
for Mr. MacDonald, the farmer,
Karl, the chauffeur, and even my Grandmother
to say, "your Father." They meant my Grandfather.

He was my Father. I was his son.
On our yearly autumn get-aways from Boston
to the family graveyard in Dunbarton,
he took the wheel himself—
like an admiral at the helm.
Freed from Karl and chuckling over the gas he was saving,
he let his motor roller-coaster
out of control down each hill.
We stopped at the *Priscilla* in Nashua
for brownies and root-beer,
and later "pumped ship" together in the Indian Summer. . . .

At the graveyard, a suave Venetian Christ
gave a sheepdog's nursing patience
to Grandfather's Aunt Lottie,
his Mother, the stone but not the bones
of his Father, Francis.
Failing as when Francis Winslow could count
them on his fingers,

the clump of virgin pine still stretched patchy ostrich necks
over the disused millpond's fragrantly woodstained water,
a reddish blur,
like the ever-blackening wine-dark coat
in our portrait of Edward Winslow
once sheriff for George the Second,
the sire of bankrupt Tories.

Grandfather and I
raked leaves from our dead forebears,
defied the dank weather
with "dragon" bonfires.

Our helper, Mr. Burroughs,
had stood with Sherman at Shiloh—
his thermos of shockless coffee
was milk and grounds;
his illegal home-made claret
was as sugary as grape jelly
in a tumbler capped with paraffin.

I borrowed Grandfather's cane
carved with the names and altitudes
of Norwegian mountains he had scaled—
more a weapon than a crutch.
I lanced it in the fauve ooze for newts.
In a tobacco tin after capture, the umber yellow mature newts
lost their leopard spots,
lay grounded as numb
as scrolls of candied grapefruit peel.
I saw myself as a young newt,
neurasthenic, scarlet
and wild in the wild coffee-colored water.

In the mornings I cuddled like a paramour
in my Grandfather's bed,
while he scouted about the chattering greenwood stove.

Grandparents

They're altogether otherworldly now,
those adults champing for their ritual Friday spin
to pharmacist and five-and-ten in Brockton.
Back in my throw-away and shaggy span
of adolescence, Grandpa still waves his stick
like a policeman;
Grandmother, like a Mohammedan, still wears her thick
lavender mourning and touring veil;
the Pierce Arrow clears its throat in a horse-stall.
Then the dry road dust rises to whiten
the fatigued elm leaves—
the nineteenth century, tired of children, is gone.
They're all gone into a world of light; the farm's my own.

The farm's my own!
Back there alone,
I keep indoors, and spoil another season.
I hear the rattley little country gramophone
racking its five foot horn:
"O Summer Time!"
Even at noon here the formidable
Ancien Régime still keeps nature at a distance. Five
green shaded light bulbs spider the billiards-table;
no field is greener than its cloth,
where Grandpa, dipping sugar for us both,
once spilled his demitasse.
His favorite ball, the number three,
still hides the coffee stain.

Never again
to walk there, chalk our cues,
insist on shooting for us both.
Grandpa! Have me, hold me, cherish me!
Tears smut my fingers. There
half my life-lease later,
I hold an *Illustrated London News*—;
disloyal still,
I doodle handlebar
mustaches on the last Russian Czar.

Commander Lowell

1887–1950

There were no undesirables or girls in my set,
when I was a boy at Mattapoisett—
only Mother, still her Father's daughter.
Her voice was still electric
with a hysterical, unmarried panic,
when she read to me from the Napoleon book.
Long-nosed Marie Louise
Hapsburg in the frontispiece
had a downright Boston bashfulness,
where she grovelled to Bonaparte, who scratched his navel,
and bolted his food—just my seven years tall!
And I, bristling and manic,
skulked in the attic,
and got two hundred French generals by name,
from *A* to *V*—from Augereau to Vandamme.
I used to dope myself asleep,
naming those unpronounceables like sheep.

Having a naval officer
for my Father was nothing to shout
about to the summer colony at "Matt."
He wasn't at all "serious,"
when he showed up on the golf course,
wearing a blue serge jacket and numbly cut
white ducks he'd bought
at a Pearl Harbor commissariat . . .
and took four shots with his putter to sink his putt.
"Bob," they said, "golf's a game you really ought to know how
    to play,
if you play at all."

They wrote him off as "naval,"
naturally supposed his sport was sailing.
Poor Father, his training was engineering!
Cheerful and cowed
among the seadogs at the Sunday yacht club,
he was never one of the crowd.

"Anchors aweigh," Daddy boomed in his bathtub,
"Anchors aweigh,"
when Lever Brothers offered to pay
him double what the Navy paid.
I nagged for his dress sword with gold braid,
and cringed because Mother, new
caps on all her teeth, was born anew
at forty. With seamanlike celerity,
Father left the Navy,
and deeded Mother his property.

He was soon fired. Year after year,
he still hummed "Anchors aweigh" in the tub—
whenever he left a job,
he bought a smarter car.
Father's last employer
was Scudder, Stevens and Clark, Investment Advisors,
himself his only client.
While Mother dragged to bed alone,
read Menninger,
and grew more and more suspicious,
he grew defiant.
Night after night,
à la clarté déserte de sa lampe,
he slid his ivory Annapolis slide rule
across a pad of graphs—
piker speculations! In three years
he squandered sixty thousand dollars.

Smiling on all,
Father was once successful enough to be lost
in the mob of ruling-class Bostonians.
As early as 1928,
he owned a house converted to oil,
and redecorated by the architect
of St. Mark's School. . . . Its main effect
was a drawing room, "longitudinal as Versailles,"
its ceiling, roughened with oatmeal, was blue as the sea.
And once
nineteen, the youngest ensign in his class,
he was "the old man" of a gunboat on the Yangtze.

Terminal Days at Beverly Farms

At Beverly Farms, a portly, uncomfortable boulder
bulked in the garden's center—
an irregular Japanese touch.
After his Bourbon "old fashioned," Father,
bronzed, breezy, a shade too ruddy,
swayed as if on deck-duty
under his six pointed star-lantern—
last July's birthday present.
He smiled his oval Lowell smile,
he wore his cream gabardine dinner-jacket,
and indigo cummerbund.
His head was efficient and hairless,
his newly dieted figure was vitally trim.

Father and Mother moved to Beverly Farms
to be a two minute walk from the station,
half an hour by train from the Boston doctors.
They had no sea-view,
but sky-blue tracks of the commuters' railroad shone
like a double-barrelled shotgun
through the scarlet late August sumac,
multiplying like cancer
at their garden's border.

Father had had two coronaries.
He still treasured underhand economies,
but his best friend was his little black *Chevie*,
garaged like a sacrificial steer
with gilded hooves,
yet sensationally sober,

and with less side than an old dancing pump.
The local dealer, a "buccaneer,"
had been bribed a "king's ransom"
to quickly deliver a car without chrome.

Each morning at eight-thirty,
inattentive and beaming,
loaded with his "calc" and "trig" books,
his clipper ship statistics,
and his ivory slide rule,
Father stole off with the *Chevie*
to loaf in the Maritime Museum at Salem.
He called the curator
"the commander of the Swiss Navy."

Father's death was abrupt and unprotesting.
His vision was still twenty-twenty.
After a morning of anxious, repetitive smiling,
his last words to Mother were:
"I feel awful."

Father's Bedroom

In my Father's bedroom:
blue threads as thin
as pen-writing on the bedspread,
blue dots on the curtains,
a blue kimono,
Chinese sandals with blue plush straps.
The broad-planked floor
had a sandpapered neatness.
The clear glass bed-lamp
with a white doily shade
was still raised a few
inches by resting on volume two
of Lafcadio Hearn's
Glimpses of unfamiliar Japan.
Its warped olive cover
was punished like a rhinoceros hide.
In the flyleaf:
"Robbie from Mother."
Years later in the same hand:
"This book has had hard usage
on the Yangtze River, China.
It was left under an open
porthole in a storm."

For Sale

Poor sheepish plaything,
organized with prodigal animosity,
lived in just a year—
my Father's cottage at Beverly Farms
was on the market the month he died.
Empty, open, intimate,
its town-house furniture
had an on tiptoe air
of waiting for the mover
on the heels of the undertaker.
Ready, afraid
of living alone till eighty,
Mother mooned in a window,
as if she had stayed on a train
one stop past her destination.

Sailing Home from Rapallo

(February 1954)

Your nurse could only speak Italian,
but after twenty minutes I could imagine your final week,
and tears ran down my cheeks. . . .

When I embarked from Italy with my Mother's body,
the whole shoreline of the *Golfo di Genova*
was breaking into fiery flower.
The crazy yellow and azure sea-sleds
blasting like jack-hammers across
the *spumante*-bubbling wake of our liner,
recalled the clashing colors of my Ford.
Mother travelled first-class in the hold;
her *Risorgimento* black and gold casket
was like Napoleon's at the *Invalides*. . . .

While the passengers were tanning
on the Mediterranean in deck-chairs,
our family cemetery in Dunbarton
lay under the White Mountains
in the sub-zero weather.
The graveyard's soil was changing to stone—
so many of its deaths had been midwinter.
Dour and dark against the blinding snowdrifts,
its black brook and fir trunks were as smooth as masts.
A fence of iron spear-hafts
black-bordered its mostly Colonial grave-slates.
The only "unhistoric" soul to come here
was Father, now buried beneath his recent
unweathered pink-veined slice of marble.
Even the Latin of his Lowell motto:

Occasionem cognosce,
seemed too businesslike and pushing here,
where the burning cold illuminated
the hewn inscriptions of Mother's relatives:
twenty or thirty Winslows and Starks.
Frost had given their names a diamond edge. . . .

In the grandiloquent lettering on Mother's coffin,
Lowell had been misspelled *LOVEL*.
The corpse
was wrapped like *panetone* in Italian tinfoil.

During Fever

All night the crib creaks;
home from the healthy country to the sick city,
my daughter in fever
flounders in her chicken-colored sleeping bag.
"Sorry," she mumbles like her dim-bulb father, "sorry."

Mother, Mother!
as a gemlike undergraduate,
part criminal and yet a Phi Bete,
I used to barge home late.
Always by the bannister
my milk-tooth mug of milk
was waiting for me on a plate
of Triskets.
Often with unadulterated joy,
Mother, we bent by the fire
rehashing Father's character—
when he thought we were asleep,
he'd tiptoe down the stairs
and chain the door.

Mother, your master-bedroom
looked away from the ocean.
You had a window-seat,
an electric blanket,
a silver hot water bottle
monogrammed like a hip-flask,
Italian china fruity
with bunches and berries
and proper *putti*.

Gold, yellow and green,
the nuptial bed
was as big as a bathroom.

Born ten years and yet an aeon
too early for the twenties,
Mother, you smile
as if you saw your Father
inches away yet hidden, as when he groused behind a screen
over a National Geographic Magazine,
whenever young men came to court you
back in those settled years of World War One.
Terrible that old life of decency
without unseemly intimacy
or quarrels, when the unemancipated woman
still had her Freudian papá and maids!

Waking in the Blue

The night attendant, a B.U. sophomore,
rouses from the mare's-nest of his drowsy head
propped on *The Meaning of Meaning*.
He catwalks down our corridor.
Azure day
makes my agonized blue window bleaker.
Crows maunder on the petrified fairway.
Absence! My heart grows tense
as though a harpoon were sparring for the kill.
(This is the house for the "mentally ill.")

What use is my sense of humor?
I grin at Stanley, now sunk in his sixties,
once a Harvard all-American fullback,
(if such were possible!)
still hoarding the build of a boy in his twenties,
as he soaks, a ramrod
with the muscle of a seal
in his long tub,
vaguely urinous from the Victorian plumbing.
A kingly granite profile in a crimson golf-cap,
worn all day, all night,
he thinks only of his figure,
of slimming on sherbet and ginger ale—
more cut off from words than a seal.

This is the way day breaks in Bowditch Hall at McLean's;
the hooded night lights bring out "Bobbie,"
Porcellian '29,
a replica of Louis XVI

without the wig—
redolent and roly-poly as a sperm whale,
as he swashbuckles about in his birthday suit
and horses at chairs.

These victorious figures of bravado ossified young.

In between the limits of day,
hours and hours go by under the crew haircuts
and slightly too little nonsensical bachelor twinkle
of the Roman Catholic attendants.
(There are no Mayflower
screwballs in the Catholic Church.)

After a hearty New England breakfast,
I weigh two hundred pounds
this morning. Cock of the walk,
I strut in my turtle-necked French sailor's jersey
before the metal shaving mirrors,
and see the shaky future grow familiar
in the pinched, indigenous faces
of these thoroughbred mental cases,
twice my age and half my weight.
We are all old-timers,
each of us holds a locked razor.

Home After Three Months Away

Gone now the baby's nurse,
a lioness who ruled the roost
and made the Mother cry.
She used to tie
gobbets of porkrind in bowknots of gauze—
three months they hung like soggy toast
on our eight foot magnolia tree,
and helped the English sparrows
weather a Boston winter.

Three months, three months!
Is Richard now himself again?
Dimpled with exaltation,
my daughter holds her levee in the tub.
Our noses rub,
each of us pats a stringy lock of hair—
they tell me nothing's gone.
Though I am forty-one,
not forty now, the time I put away
was child's-play. After thirteen weeks
my child still dabs her cheeks
to start me shaving. When
we dress her in her sky-blue corduroy,
she changes to a boy,
and floats my shaving brush
and washcloth in the flush. . . .
Dearest, I cannot loiter here
in lather like a polar bear.

Recuperating, I neither spin nor toil.
Three stories down below,
a choreman tends our coffin's length of soil,
and seven horizontal tulips blow.
Just twelve months ago,
these flowers were pedigreed
imported Dutchmen; now no one need
distinguish them from weed.
Bushed by the late spring snow,
they cannot meet
another year's snowballing enervation.

I keep no rank nor station.
Cured, I am frizzled, stale and small.

II

Memories of West Street and Lepke

Only teaching on Tuesdays, book-worming
in pajamas fresh from the washer each morning,
I hog a whole house on Boston's
"hardly passionate Marlborough Street,"
where even the man
scavenging filth in the back alley trash cans,
has two children, a beach wagon, a helpmate,
and is a "young Republican."
I have a nine months' daughter,
young enough to be my granddaughter.
Like the sun she rises in her flame-flamingo infants' wear.

These are the tranquillized *Fifties*,
and I am forty. Ought I to regret my seedtime?
I was a fire-breathing Catholic C.O.,
and made my manic statement,
telling off the state and president, and then
sat waiting sentence in the bull pen
beside a Negro boy with curlicues
of marijuana in his hair.

Given a year,
I walked on the roof of the West Street Jail, a short
enclosure like my school soccer court,
and saw the Hudson River once a day
through sooty clothesline entanglements
and bleaching khaki tenements.
Strolling, I yammered metaphysics with Abramowitz,
a jaundice-yellow ("it's really tan")
and fly-weight pacifist,

so vegetarian,
he wore rope shoes and preferred fallen fruit.
He tried to convert Bioff and Brown,
the Hollywood pimps, to his diet.
Hairy, muscular, suburban,
wearing chocolate double-breasted suits,
they blew their tops and beat him black and blue.

I was so out of things, I'd never heard
of the Jehovah's Witnesses.
"Are you a C.O.?" I asked a fellow jailbird.
"No," he answered, "I'm a J.W."
He taught me the "hospital tuck,"
and pointed out the T-shirted back
of *Murder Incorporated's* Czar Lepke,
there piling towels on a rack,
or dawdling off to his little segregated cell full
of things forbidden the common man:
a portable radio, a dresser, two toy American
flags tied together with a ribbon of Easter palm.
Flabby, bald, lobotomized,
he drifted in a sheepish calm,
where no agonizing reappraisal
jarred his concentration on the electric chair—
hanging like an oasis in his air
of lost connections. . . .

Man and Wife

Tamed by *Miltown*, we lie on Mother's bed;
the rising sun in war paint dyes us red;
in broad daylight her gilded bed-posts shine,
abandoned, almost Dionysian.
At last the trees are green on Marlborough Street,
blossoms on our magnolia ignite
the morning with their murderous five days' white.
All night I've held your hand,
as if you had
a fourth time faced the kingdom of the mad—
its hackneyed speech, its homicidal eye—
and dragged me home alive. . . . Oh my *Petite*,
clearest of all God's creatures, still all air and nerve:
you were in your twenties, and I,
once hand on glass
and heart in mouth,
outdrank the Rahvs in the heat
of Greenwich Village, fainting at your feet—
too boiled and shy
and poker-faced to make a pass,
while the shrill verve
of your invective scorched the traditional South.

Now twelve years later, you turn your back.
Sleepless, you hold
your pillow to your hollows like a child;
your old-fashioned tirade—
loving, rapid, merciless—
breaks like the Atlantic Ocean on my head.

"To Speak of Woe That Is in Marriage"

"It is the future generation that presses into being by means of these exuberant feelings and supersensible soap bubbles of ours."   SCHOPENHAUER

"The hot night makes us keep our bedroom windows open.
Our magnolia blossoms. Life begins to happen.
My hopped up husband drops his home disputes,
and hits the streets to cruise for prostitutes,
free-lancing out along the razor's edge.
This screwball might kill his wife, then take the pledge.
Oh the monotonous meanness of his lust. . . .
It's the injustice . . . he is so unjust—
whiskey-blind, swaggering home at five.
My only thought is how to keep alive.
What makes him tick? Each night now I tie
ten dollars and his car key to my thigh. . . .
Gored by the climacteric of his want,
he stalls above me like an elephant."

Skunk Hour

(FOR ELIZABETH BISHOP)

Nautilus Island's hermit
heiress still lives through winter in her Spartan cottage;
her sheep still graze above the sea.
Her son's a bishop. Her farmer
is first selectman in our village;
she's in her dotage.

Thirsting for
the hierarchic privacy
of Queen Victoria's century,
she buys up all
the eyesores facing her shore,
and lets them fall.

The season's ill—
we've lost our summer millionaire,
who seemed to leap from an L. L. Bean
catalogue. His nine-knot yawl
was auctioned off to lobstermen.
A red fox stain covers Blue Hill.

And now our fairy
decorator brightens his shop for fall;
his fishnet's filled with orange cork,
orange, his cobbler's bench and awl;
there is no money in his work,
he'd rather marry.

One dark night,
my Tudor Ford climbed the hill's skull;

I watched for love-cars. Lights turned down,
they lay together, hull to hull,
where the graveyard shelves on the town. . . .
My mind's not right.

A car radio bleats,
"Love, O careless Love. . . ." I hear
my ill-spirit sob in each blood cell,
as if my hand were at its throat. . . .
I myself am hell;
nobody's here—

only skunks, that search
in the moonlight for a bite to eat.
They march on their soles up Main Street:
white stripes, moonstruck eyes' red fire
under the chalk-dry and spar spire
of the Trinitarian Church.

I stand on top
of our back steps and breathe the rich air—
a mother skunk with her column of kittens swills the garbage pail.
She jabs her wedge-head in a cup
of sour cream, drops her ostrich tail,
and will not scare.

For the Union Dead

For my friend,
WILLIAM ALFRED

NOTE

I want to make a few admissions and disclosures. My poems on
Hawthorne and Edwards draw heavily on prose sentences by
their subjects. "The Scream" owes everything to Elizabeth
Bishop's beautiful, calm story, *In the Village*. "The Lesson" picks
up a phrase or two from Rafael Alberti. "Returning" was sug-
gested by Giuseppi Ungaretti's "Canzone." "The Public Garden"
is a recasting and clarification of an old confusing poem of mine
called "David and Bathsheba in the Public Garden." "Beyond the
Alps" is the poem I published in *Life Studies*, but with a stanza
restored at the suggestion of John Berryman. "Florence" steals a
sentence from Mary McCarthy's book on Florence. Poems in this
book have appeared in Partisan Review, the London Observer,
Encounter, Kenyon Review, Yale Review, The Atlantic, Poetry,
and The New York Review of Books. The poem "Hawthorne"
was written for the Centenary Edition of the works of Nathaniel
Hawthorne (Ohio State University Press).

R.L.

Water

It was a Maine lobster town—
each morning boatloads of hands
pushed off for granite
quarries on the islands,

and left dozens of bleak
white frame houses stuck
like oyster shells
on a hill of rock,

and below us, the sea lapped
the raw little match-stick
mazes of a weir,
where the fish for bait were trapped.

Remember? We sat on a slab of rock.
From this distance in time,
it seems the color
of iris, rotting and turning purpler,

but it was only
the usual gray rock
turning the usual green
when drenched by the sea.

The sea drenched the rock
at our feet all day,
and kept tearing away
flake after flake.

One night you dreamed
you were a mermaid clinging to a wharf-pile,
and trying to pull
off the barnacles with your hands.

We wished our two souls
might return like gulls
to the rock. In the end,
the water was too cold for us.

The Old Flame

My old flame, my wife!
Remember our lists of birds?
One morning last summer, I drove
by our house in Maine. It was still
on top of its hill—

Now a red ear of Indian maize
was splashed on the door.
Old Glory with thirteen stripes
hung on a pole. The clapboard
was old-red schoolhouse red.

Inside, a new landlord,
a new wife, a new broom!
Atlantic seaboard antique shop
pewter and plunder
shone in each room.

A new frontier!
No running next door
now to phone the sheriff
for his taxi to Bath
and the State Liquor Store!

No one saw your ghostly
imaginary lover
stare through the window,
and tighten
the scarf at his throat.

Health to the new people,
health to their flag, to their old
restored house on the hill!
Everything had been swept bare,
furnished, garnished and aired.

Everything's changed for the best—
how quivering and fierce we were,
there snowbound together,
simmering like wasps
in our tent of books!

Poor ghost, old love, speak
with your old voice
of flaming insight
that kept us awake all night.
In one bed and apart,

we heard the plow
groaning up hill—
a red light, then a blue,
as it tossed off the snow
to the side of the road.

Middle Age

Now the midwinter grind
is on me, New York
drills through my nerves,
as I walk
the chewed-up streets.

At forty-five,
what next, what next?
At every corner,
I meet my Father,
my age, still alive.

Father, forgive me
my injuries,
as I forgive
those I
have injured!

You never climbed
Mount Sion, yet left
dinosaur
death-steps on the crust,
where I must walk.

The Scream

(derived from Elizabeth Bishop's story *In the Village*)

A scream, the echo of a scream,
now only a thinning echo . . .
As a child in Nova Scotia,
I used to watch the sky,
Swiss sky, too blue, too dark.

A cow drooled green grass strings,
made cow flop, *smack, smack, smack!*
and tried to brush off its flies
on a lilac bush—all,
forever, at one fell swoop!

In the blacksmith's shop,
the horseshoes sailed through the dark,
like bloody little moons,
red-hot, hissing, protesting,
as they drowned in the pan.

Back and away and back!
Mother kept coming and going—
with me, without me!
Mother's dresses were black
or white, or black-and-white.

One day she changed to purple,
and left her mourning. At the fitting,
the dressmaker crawled on the floor,
eating pins, like Nebuchadnezzar
on his knees eating grass.

Drummers sometimes came
selling gilded red
and green books, unlovely books!
The people in the pictures
wore clothes like the purple dress.

Later, she gave the scream,
not even loud at first . . .
When she went away I thought
"But you can't love everyone,
your heart won't let you!"

A scream! But they are all gone,
those aunts and aunts, a grandfather,
a grandmother, my mother—
even her scream—too frail
for us to hear their voices long.

The Mouth of the Hudson

(FOR ESTHER BROOKS)

A single man stands like a bird-watcher,
and scuffles the pepper and salt snow
from a discarded, gray
Westinghouse Electric cable drum.
He cannot discover America by counting
the chains of condemned freight-trains
from thirty states. They jolt and jar
and junk in the siding below him.
He has trouble with his balance.
His eyes drop,
and he drifts with the wild ice
ticking seaward down the Hudson,
like the blank sides of a jig-saw puzzle.

The ice ticks seaward like a clock.
A Negro toasts
wheat-seeds over the coke-fumes
of a punctured barrel.
Chemical air
sweeps in from New Jersey,
and smells of coffee.

Across the river,
ledges of suburban factories tan
in the sulphur-yellow sun
of the unforgivable landscape.

Fall 1961

Back and forth, back and forth
goes the tock, tock, tock
of the orange, bland, ambassadorial
face of the moon
on the grandfather clock.

All autumn, the chafe and jar
of nuclear war;
we have talked our extinction to death.
I swim like a minnow
behind my studio window.

Our end drifts nearer,
the moon lifts,
radiant with terror.
The state
is a diver under a glass bell.

A father's no shield
for his child.
We are like a lot of wild
spiders crying together,
but without tears.

Nature holds up a mirror.
One swallow makes a summer.
It's easy to tick
off the minutes,
but the clockhands stick.

Back and forth!
Back and forth, back and forth—
my one point of rest
is the orange and black
oriole's swinging nest!

Florence

(FOR MARY McCARTHY)

I long for the black ink,
cuttlefish, April, Communists
and brothels of Florence—
everything, even the British
fairies who haunted the hills,
even the chills and fever
that came once a month
and forced me to think.
The apple was more human there than here,
but it took a long time for the blinding
golden rind to mellow.

How vulnerable the horseshoe crabs
dredging the bottom like flat-irons
in their antique armor,
with their swordgrass blackbone tails,
made for a child to grab
and throw strangling ashore!

Oh Florence, Florence, patroness
of the lovely tyranicides!
Where the tower of the Old Palace
pierces the sky
like a hypodermic needle,
Perseus, David and Judith,
lords and ladies of the Blood,
Greek demi-gods of the Cross,
rise sword in hand
above the unshaven,
formless decapitation

of the monsters, tubs of guts,
mortifying chunks for the pack.
Pity the monsters!
Pity the monsters!
Perhaps, one always took the wrong side—
Ah, to have known, to have loved
too many Davids and Judiths!
My heart bleeds black blood for the monster.
I have seen the Gorgon.
The erotic terror
of her helpless, big bosomed body
lay like slop.
Wall-eyed, staring the despot to stone,
her severed head swung
like a lantern in the victor's hand.

The Lesson

No longer to lie reading *Tess of the d'Urbervilles*,
while the high, mysterious squirrels
rain small green branches on our sleep!

All that landscape, one likes to think it died
or slept with us, that we ourselves died
or slept then in the age and second of our habitation.

The green leaf cushions the same dry footprint,
or the child's boat luffs in the same dry chop,
and we are where we were. We were!

Perhaps the trees stopped growing in summer amnesia;
their day that gave them veins is rooted down—
and the nights? They are for sleeping now as then.

Ah the light lights the window of my young night,
and you never turn off the light,
while the books lie in the library, and go on reading.

The barberry berry sticks on the small hedge,
cold slits the same crease in the finger,
the same thorn hurts. The leaf repeats the lesson.

Those Before Us

They are all outline, uniformly gray,
unregenerate arrowheads sloughed up by the path here,
or in the corners of the eye, they play
their thankless, fill-in roles. They never were.

Wormwood on the veranda! Plodding needles
still prod the coarse pink yarn into a dress.
The muskrat that took a slice of your thumb still huddles,
a mop of hair and a heart-beat on the porch—

there's the tin wastebasket where it learned to wait
for us playing dead, the slats it mashed in terror,
its spoor of cornflakes, and the packing crate
it furiously slashed to matchwood to escape.

Their chairs were *ex cathedra*, yet if you draw back the blinds,
(as full of windows as a fishnet now)
you will hear them conspiring, slapping hands
across the bent card-table, still leaf-green.

Vacations, stagnant growth. But in the silence,
some one lets out his belt to breathe, some one
roams in negligee. Bless the confidence
of their sitting unguarded there in stocking feet.

Sands drop from the hour-glass waist and swallow tail.
We follow their gunshy shadows down the trail—
those before us! Pardon them for existing.
We have stopped watching them. They have stopped watching.

Eye and Tooth

My whole eye was sunset red,
the old cut cornea throbbed,
I saw things darkly,
as through an unwashed goldfish globe.

I lay all day on my bed.
I chain-smoked through the night,
learning to flinch
at the flash of the matchlight.

Outside, the summer rain,
a simmer of rot and renewal,
fell in pinpricks.
Even new life is fuel.

My eyes throb.
Nothing can dislodge
the house with my first tooth
noosed in a knot to the doorknob.

Nothing can dislodge
the triangular blotch
of rot on the red roof,
a cedar hedge, or the shade of a hedge.

No ease from the eye
of the sharp-shinned hawk in the birdbook there,
with reddish brown buffalo hair
on its shanks, one ascetic talon

clasping the abstract imperial sky.
It says:
an eye for an eye,
a tooth for a tooth.

No ease for the boy at the keyhole,
his telescope,
when the women's white bodies flashed
in the bathroom. Young, my eyes began to fail.

Nothing! No oil
for the eye, nothing to pour
on those waters or flames.
I am tired. Everyone's tired of my turmoil.

Alfred Corning Clark

(1916–1961)

You read the *New York Times*
every day at recess,
but in its dry
obituary, a list
of your wives, nothing is news,
except the ninety-five
thousand dollar engagement ring
you gave the sixth.
Poor rich boy,
you were unreasonably adult
at taking your time,
and died at forty-five.
Poor Al Clark,
behind your enlarged,
hardly recognizable photograph,
I feel the pain.
You were alive. You are dead.
You wore bow-ties and dark
blue coats, and sucked
wintergreen or cinnamon lifesavers
to sweeten your breath.
There must be something—
some one to praise
your triumphant diffidence,
your refusal of exertion,
the intelligence
that pulsed in the sensitive,
pale concavities of your forehead.
You never worked,
and were third in the form.

I owe you something—
I was befogged,
and you were too bored,
quick and cool to laugh.
You are dear to me, Alfred;
our reluctant souls united
in our unconventional
illegal games of chess
on the St. Mark's quadrangle.
You usually won—
motionless
as a lizard in the sun.

Child's Song

My cheap toy lamp
gives little light
all night, all night,
when my muscles cramp.

Sometimes I touch your hand
across my cot,
and our fingers knot,
but there's no hand

to take me home—
no Carribean
island, where even
the shark is at home.

It must be heaven.
There on that island
the white sand shines
like a birchwood fire.

Help, saw me in two,
put me on the shelf!
Sometimes the little muddler
can't stand itself!

Epigram

(FOR HANNAH ARENDT)

Think of Leonidas perhaps and the hoplites
glittering with liberation,
as they combed one another's golden Botticellian
hair at Thermopylae—friends and lovers,
the bride and the bridegroom—
and moved into position to die.

Law

Under one law,
or two,
to lie unsleeping,
still sleeping on the battlefield . . .

On Sunday mornings,
I used to foray
bass-plugging out of season on
the posted reservoirs.

Outside the law.
At every bend I saw
only the looping shore
of nature's monotonous backlash.

The same. The same.
Then once, in a flash,
fresh ground, though trodden,
a man-made landscape.

A Norman canal
shot through razored green lawns;
black reflecting water arched
little sky-hung bridges of unhewn stone—

outside the law:
black, gray, green and blue,
water, stone, grass and sky,
and each unique set stone!

The Public Garden

Burnished, burned-out, still burning as the year
you lead me to our stamping ground.
The city and its cruising cars surround
the Public Garden. All's alive—
the children crowding home from school at five,
punting a football in the bricky air,
the sailors and their pick-ups under trees
with Latin labels. And the jaded flock
of swanboats paddles to its dock.
The park is drying.
Dead leaves thicken to a ball
inside the basin of a fountain, where
the heads of four stone lions stare
and suck on empty fawcets. Night
deepens. From the arched bridge, we see
the shedding park-bound mallards, how they keep
circling and diving in the lanternlight,
searching for something hidden in the muck.
And now the moon, earth's friend, that cared so much
for us, and cared so little, comes again—
always a stranger! As we walk,
it lies like chalk
over the waters. Everything's aground.
Remember summer? Bubbles filled
the fountain, and we splashed. We drowned
in Eden, while Jehovah's grass-green lyre
was rustling all about us in the leaves
that gurgled by us, turning upside down . . .
The fountain's failing waters flash around
the garden. Nothing catches fire.

Lady Ralegh's Lament

1618

Sir Walter, oh, oh, my own Sir Walter—
the sour Tower and the Virgin Queen's garden close
are deflowered and gone now . . .
Horrible the connoisseur tyrant's querulous strut;
an acorn dances in a girdle of green oak leaves
up the steps to the scaffold to the block,
square bastard of an oak. Clearly, clearly,
the Atlantic whitens to merge Sir Walter's head,
still dangling in its scarlet, tangled twine,
as if beseeching voyage. Voyage?
Down and down; the compass needle dead on terror.

Going to and fro

It's authentic perhaps
to have been there, if now
you could loll on the ledge for a moment,
sunning like a couple,
and look down at the gaps—
if you could for a moment . . .

One step, two steps, three steps:
the hot-dog and coca cola bar,
the Versailles steps,
the Puritan statue—
if you could get through the Central Park
by counting . . .

But the intestines shiver,
the ferry saloon thugs with your pain
across the river—pain,
suffering without purgation,
the back-track of the screw.
But you had instants,

to give the devil his due—
he and you
once dug it all out of the dark
unconscious bowels of the nerves:
pure gold, the root of evil,
sunshine that gave the day a scheme.

And now? Ah Lucifer!
how often you wanted your fling

with those French girls, Mediterranean
luminaries, Mary, Myrtho, Isis—
as far out as the sphynx!
The love that moves the stars

moved you!
It set you going to and fro
and up and down—
If you could get loose
from the earth by counting
your steps to the noose . . .

Myopia: a Night

Bed, glasses off, and all's
ramshackle, streaky, weird
for the near-sighted, just
a foot away.
　　　　　The light's
still on an instant. Here
are the blurred titles, here
the books are blue hills, browns,
greens, fields, or color.
　　　　　　　　This
is the departure strip,
the dream-road. Whoever built it
left numbers, words and arrows.
He had to leave in a hurry.

I see
a dull and alien room,
my cell of learning,
white, brightened by white pipes,
ramrods of steam . . . I hear
the lonely metal breathe
and gurgle like the sick.
And yet my eyes avoid
that room. No need to see.
No need to know I hoped
its blank, foregoing whiteness
would burn away the blur,
as my five senses clenched
their teeth, thought stitched to thought,
as through a needle's eye . . .

I see the morning star . . .

Think of him in the Garden,
that seed of wisdom, Eve's
seducer, stuffed with man's
corruption, stuffed with triumph:
Satan triumphant in
the Garden! In a moment,
all that blinding brightness
changed into a serpent,
lay grovelling on its gut.

What has disturbed this household?
Only a foot away,
the familiar faces blur.
At fifty we're so fragile,
a feather . . .

The things of the eye are done.
On the illuminated black dial,
green ciphers of a new moon—
one, two, three, four, five, six!
I breathe and cannot sleep.
Then morning comes,
saying, "This was a night."

Returning

Homecoming to the sheltered little resort,
where the members of my gang
are bald-headed, in business,
and the dogs still know me by my smell . . .
It's rather a dead town
after my twenty years' mirage.

Long awash,
breaking myself against the surf,
touching bottom, rushed
by the green go-light
of those nervous waters, I found
my exhaustion, the light of the world.

Nothing is deader than this small town main street,
where the venerable elm sickens, and hardens
with tarred cement, where no leaf
is born, or falls, or resists till winter.

But I remember its former fertility,
how everything came out clearly
in the hour of credulity
and young summer, when this street
was already somewhat overshaded,
and here at the altar of surrender,
I met you,
the death of thirst in my brief flesh.

That was the first growth,
the heir of all my minutes,

the victim of every ramification—
more and more it grew green, and gave too much shelter.

And now at my homecoming,
the barked elms stand up like sticks along the street.
I am a foot taller than when I left,
and cannot see the dirt at my feet.

Yet sometimes I catch my vague mind
circling with a glazed eye
for a name without a face, or a face without a name,
and at every step,
I startle them. They start up,
dog-eared, bald as baby birds.

The Drinker

The man is killing time—there's nothing else.
No help now from the fifth of Bourbon
chucked helter-skelter into the river,
even its cork sucked under.

Stubbed before-breakfast cigarettes
burn bull's-eyes on the bedside table;
a plastic tumbler of alka seltzer
champagnes in the bathroom.

No help from his body, the whale's
warm-hearted blubber, foundering down
leagues of ocean, gasping whiteness.
The barbed hooks fester. The lines snap tight.

When he looks for neighbors, their names blur in the window,
his distracted eye sees only glass sky.
His despair has the galvanized color
of the mop and water in the galvanized bucket.

Once she was close to him
as water to the dead metal.

He looks at her engagements inked on her calendar.
A list of indictments.
At the numbers in her thumbed black telephone book.
A quiver full of arrows.

Her absence hisses like steam,
the pipes sing . . .

even corroded metal somehow functions.
He snores in his iron lung,

and hears the voice of Eve,
beseeching freedom from the Garden's
perfect and ponderous bubble. No voice
outsings the serpent's flawed, euphoric hiss.

The cheese wilts in the rat-trap,
the milk turns to junket in the cornflakes bowl,
car keys and razor blades
shine in an ashtray.

Is he killing time? Out on the street,
two cops on horseback clop through the April rain
to check the parking meter violations—
their oilskins yellow as forsythia.

Hawthorne

Follow its lazy main street lounging
from the alms house to Gallows Hill
along a flat, unvaried surface
covered with wooden houses
aged by yellow drain
like the unhealthy hair of an old dog.
You'll walk to no purpose
in Hawthorne's Salem.

I cannot resilver the smudged plate.

I drop to Hawthorne, the customs officer,
measuring coal and mostly trying to keep warm—
to the stunted black schooner,
the dismal South-end dock,
the wharf-piles with their fungus of ice.
On State Street
a steeple with a glowing dial-clock
measures the weary hours,
the merciless march of professional feet.

Even this shy distrustful ego
sometimes walked on top of the blazing roof,
and felt those flashes
that char the discharged cells of the brain.

Look at the faces—
Longfellow, Lowell, Holmes and Whittier!
Study the grizzled silver of their beards.
Hawthorne's picture,

however, has a blond mustache
and golden General Custer scalp.
He looks like a Civil War officer.
He shines in the firelight. His hard
survivor's smile is touched with fire.

Leave him alone for a moment or two,
and you'll see him with his head
bent down, brooding, brooding,
eyes fixed on some chip,
some stone, some common plant,
the commonest thing,
as if it were the clue.
The disturbed eyes rise,
furtive, foiled, dissatisfied
from meditation on the true
and insignificant.

Jonathan Edwards in Western Massachusetts

Edwards' great millstone and rock
of hope has crumbled, but the square
white houses of his flock
stand in the open air,

out in the cold,
like sheep outside the fold.
Hope lives in doubt.
Faith is trying to do without

faith. In western Massachusetts,
I could almost feel the frontier
crack and disappear.
Edwards thought the world would end there.

We know how the world will end,
but where is paradise, each day farther
from the Pilgrim's blues for England
and the Promised Land.

Was it some country house
that seemed as if it were
Whitehall, if the Lord were there?
so nobly did he live.

Gardens designed
that the breath of flowers in the wind,
or crushed underfoot,
came and went like warbling music?

Bacon's great oak grove
he refused to sell,
when he fell,
saying, "Why should I sell my feathers?"

Ah paradise! Edwards,
I would be afraid
to meet you there as a shade.
We move in different circles.

As a boy, you built a booth
in a swamp for prayer;
lying on your back,
you saw the spiders fly,

basking at their ease,
swimming from tree to tree—
so high, they seemed tacked to the sky.
You knew they would die.

Poor country Berkeley at Yale,
you saw the world was soul,
the soul of God! The soul
of Sarah Pierrepont!

So filled with delight in the Great Being,
she hardly cared for anything—
walking the fields, sweetly singing,
conversing with some one invisible.

Then God's love shone in sun, moon and stars,
on earth, in the waters,
in the air, in the loose winds,
which used to greatly fix your mind.

Often she saw you come home from a ride
or a walk, your coat dotted with thoughts
you had pinned there
on slips of paper.

You gave
her Pompey, a Negro slave,
and eleven children.
Yet people were spiders

in your moment of glory,
at the Great Awakening—"Alas, how many
in this very meeting house are more than likely
to remember my discourse in hell!"

The meeting house remembered!
You stood on stilts in the air,
but you fell from your parish.
"All rising is by a winding stair."

On my pilgrimage to Northampton,
I found no relic,
except the round slice of an oak
you are said to have planted.

It was flesh-colored, new,
and a common piece of kindling,
only fit for burning.
You too must have been green once.

White wig and black coat,
all cut from one cloth,
and designed
like your mind!

I love you faded,
old, exiled and afraid
to leave your last flock, a dozen
Houssatonic Indian children;

afraid to leave
all your writing, writing, writing,
denying the Freedom of the Will.
You were afraid to be president

of Princeton, and wrote:
"My deffects are well known;
I have a constitution
peculiarly unhappy:

flaccid solids,
vapid, sizzy, scarse fluids,
causing a childish weakness,
a low tide of spirits.

I am contemptible,
stiff and dull.

Why should I leave behind
my delight and entertainment,
those studies
that have swallowed up my mind?"

Tenth Muse

Tenth Muse, Oh my heart-felt Sloth,
how often now you come to my bed,
thin as a canvas in your white and red
check dresses like a table cloth,
my Dearest, settling like my shroud!

Yes, yes, I ought to remember Moses
jogging down on his mule from the Mount
with the old law, the old mistake,
safe in his saddlebags, and chiselled
on the stones we cannot bear or break.

Here waiting, here waiting for an answer
from this malignant surf of unopened letters,
always reaching land too late,
as fact and abstraction accumulate,
and the signature fades from the paper—

I like to imagine it must have been simpler
in the days of Lot,
or when Greek and Roman picturebook
gods sat combing their golden beards,
each on his private hill or mountain.

But I suppose even God was born
too late to trust the old religion—
all those settings out
that never left the ground,
beginning in wisdom, dying in doubt.

The Neo-Classical Urn

I rub my head and find a turtle shell
stuck on a pole,
each hair electrical
with charges, and the juice alive
with ferment. Bubbles drive
the motor, always purposeful . . .
Poor head!
How its skinny shell once hummed,
as I sprinted down the colonnade
of bleaching pines, cylindrical
clipped trunks without a twig between them. Rest!
I could not rest. At full run on the curve,
I left the caste stone statue of a nymph,
her soaring armpits and her one bare breast,
gray from the rain and graying in the shade,
as on, on, in sun, the pathway now a dyke,
I swerved between two water bogs,
two seins of moss, and stooped to snatch
the painted turtles on dead logs.
In that season of joy,
my turtle catch
was thirty-three,
dropped splashing in our garden urn,
like money in the bank,
the plop and splash
of turtle on turtle,
fed raw gobs of hash . . .

Oh neo-classical white urn, Oh nymph,
Oh lute! The boy was pitiless who strummed

their elegy,
for as the month wore on,
the turtles rose,
and popped up dead on the stale scummed
surface—limp wrinkled heads and legs withdrawn
in pain. What pain? A turtle's nothing. No
grace, no cerebration, less free will
than the mosquito I must kill—
nothings! Turtles! I rub my skull,
that turtle shell,
and breathe their dying smell,
still watch their crippled last survivors pass,
and hobble humpbacked through the grizzled grass.

Caligula

My namesake, Little Boots, Caligula,
you disappoint me. Tell me what I saw
to make me like you when we met at school?
I took your name—poor odd-ball, poor spoiled fool,
my prince, young innocent and bowdlerized!
Your true face sneers at me, mean, thin, agonized,
the rusty Roman medal where I see
my lowest depths of possibility.

What can be salvaged from your life? A pain
that gently darkens over heart and brain,
a fairy's touch, a cobweb's weight of pain,
now makes me tremble at your right to live.
I live your last night. Sleepless fugitive,
your purple bedclothes and imperial eagle
grow so familiar they are home. Your regal
hand accepts my hand. You bend my wrist,
and tear the tendons with your strangler's twist . . .
You stare down hallways, mile on stoney mile,
where statues of the gods return your smile.
Why did you smash their heads and give them yours?
You hear your household panting on all fours,
and itemize your features—sleep's old aide!
Item: your body hairy, badly made,
head hairless, smoother than your marble head;
Item: eyes hollow, hollow temples, red
cheeks rough with rouge, legs spindly, hands that leave
a clammy snail's trail on your soggy sleeve . . .
a hand no hand will hold . . . nose thin, thin neck—
you wish the Romans had a single neck!

Small thing, where are you? Child, you sucked your thumb,
and could not sleep unless you hugged the numb
and wooly-witted toys of your small zoo.
There was some reason then to fondle you
before you found the death-mask for your play.
Lie very still, sleep with clasped hands, and pray
for nothing, Child! Think, even at the end,
good dreams were faithful. You betray no friend
now that no animal will share your bed.
Don't think! . . . And yet the God Adonis bled
and lay beside you, forcing you to strip.
You felt his gored thigh spurting on your hip.
Your mind burned, you were God, a thousand plans
ran zig-zag, zig-zag. You began to dance
for joy, and called your menials to arrange
deaths for the gods. You worshipped your great change,
took a cold bath, and rolled your genitals
until they shrank to marbles . . .

Animals
fattened for your arena suffered less
than you in dying—yours the lawlessness
of something simple that has lost its law,
my namesake, and the last Caligula.

The Severed Head

Shoes off and necktie, hunting the desired
butterfly here and there without success,
I let nostalgia drown me. I was tired
of pencilling the darker passages,
and let my ponderous Bible strike the floor.
My house was changing to a lost address,
the nameplate fell like a horse-shoe from the door,
where someone, hitting nails into a board,
had set his scaffolding. I heard him pour
mortar to seal the outlets, as I snored,
watching the knobbed, brown, wooden chandelier,
slicing the silence on a single cord.
In the low sun, about to disappear,
each branch was like a stocking-stretcher, cut
into a gryphon clawing upward. Here
and there, dull guilding pocked a talon. What
I imagined was a spider crab, my small
chance of surviving in this room. Its shut
windows had sunken into solid wall.
I nursed my last clear breath of oxygen,
there, waiting for the chandelier to fall,
tentacles clawing for my jugular. Then
a man came toward me with a manuscript,
scratching in last revisions with a pen
that left no markings on the page, yet dripped
a red ink dribble on us, as he pressed
the little strip of plastic tubing clipped
to feed it from his heart. His hand caressed
my hand a moment, settled like a toad,
lay clammy, comfortable, helpless, and at rest,

although his veins seemed pulsing to explode.
His suit was brushed and pressed too savagely;
one sleeve was shorter than his shirt, and showed
a glassy cuff-link with a butterfly
inside. Nothing about him seemed to match,
and yet I saw the bouillon of his eye
was the same color as his frayed mustache,
too brown, too bushy, lifted from an age
when people wore mustaches. On each lash,
a tear had snowballed. Then he shook his page,
tore it to pieces, and began to twist
and trample on the mangle in his rage.

"Sometimes I ask myself, if I exist,"
he grumbled, and I saw a sheet of glass
had fallen inches from us, and just missed
halving our bodies, and behind it grass-
green water flushed the glass, and fast fish stirred
and panted, ocean butterflies. A mass
of shadows followed them like moths, and blurred
tentacles, thirsting for a drop of life,
panted with calm inertia. Then I heard
my friend unclasp a rusty pocket-knife.
He cut out squares of paper, made a stack,
and formed the figure of his former wife:
Square head, square feet, square hands, square breasts, square back.

He left me. While the light began to fail,
I read my Bible till the page turned black.
The pitying, brute, doughlike face of Jael
watched me with sad inertia, as I read—
Jael hammering and hammering her nail
through Sisera's idolatrous, nailed head.

Her folded dress lay underneath my head.

Beyond the Alps

"Au delà les Alpes est l'Italie," Napoleon 1797

(ON THE TRAIN FROM ROME TO PARIS, 1950, THE YEAR PIUS XII
DEFINED THE DOGMA OF MARY'S BODILY ASSUMPTION)

Reading how even the Swiss had thrown the sponge
in once again, and Everest was still
unscaled, I watched our Paris pullman lunge,
mooning across the fallow Alpine snow—
O bella Roma! I saw our stewards go
foreward on tiptoe banging on their gongs.
Man changed to landscape. Much against my will,
I left the City of God where it belongs.
There the skirt-mad Mussolini unfurled
the eagle of Caesar. He was one of us
only, pure prose. I envy the conspicuous
waste of our grandparents on their grand tours—
long-haired Victorian sages accepted the universe,
while breezing on their trust funds through the world.

When the Vatican made Mary's Assumption dogma,
the crowds at San Pietro screamed *Papa!*
The Holy Father dropped his shaving glass,
and listened. His electric razor purred,
his pet canary chirped on his right hand.
The lights of science couldn't hold a candle
to Mary risen, gorgeous as a jungle bird!
But who believed this? Who could understand?
Pilgrims still kissed Saint Peter's brazen sandal.
The Duce's lynched, bare, booted skull still spoke.
God herded his people to the *coup de grace*—

the costumed Switzers sloped their pikes to push.
Oh Pius, through the monstrous human crush . . .

I thought of Ovid. For in Caesar's eyes
that tomcat had the Number of the Beast,
and now where Turkey faces the red east,
and the twice-stormed Crimean spit, he cries:
"Rome asked for poets. At her beck and call,
came Lucan, Tacitus and Juvenal,
the *black republicans* who tore the tits
and bowels of the Mother Wolf to bits—
Then psychopath and soldier waved the rod
of empire over Caesar's salvaged bog . . .
Imperial Tiber, Oh my yellow dog,
black earth by the black Roman sea, I lie
with the boy-crazy daughter of the God,
il Duce Augusto. I shall never die."

Our mountain-climbing train had come to earth.
Tired of the querulous hush-hush of the wheels,
the blear-eyed ego kicking in my berth
lay still, and saw Apollo plant his heels
on terra firma through the morning's thigh—
each backward wasted Alp, a Parthenon,
fire-branded socket of the cyclops' eye . . .
There are no tickets to that altitude,
once held by Hellas when the Goddess stood,
prince, pope, philosopher and golden bough,
pure mind and murder at the scything prow—
Minerva the mis-carriage of the brain . . .

Now Paris, our black classic, breaking up
like killer kings on an Etruscan cup.

July in Washington

The stiff spokes of this wheel
touch the sore spots of the earth.

On the Potomac, swan-white
power launches keep breasting the sulphurous wave.

Otters slide and dive and slick back their hair,
raccoons clean their meat in the creek.

On the circles, green statues ride like South American
liberators above the breeding vegetation—

prongs and spearheads of some equatorial
backland that will inherit the globe.

The elect, the elected . . . they come here bright as dimes,
and die dishevelled and soft.

We cannot name their names, or number their dates—
circle on circle, like rings on a tree—

but we wish the river had another shore,
some further range of delectable mountains,

distant hills powdered blue as a girl's eyelid.
It seems the least little shove would land us there,

that only the slightest repugnance of our bodies
we no longer control could drag us back.

Buenos Aires

In my room at the Hotel Continentál
a thousand miles from nowhere,
I heard
the bulky, beefy breathing of the herds.

Cattle furnished my new clothes:
my coat of limp, chestnut-colored suede,
my sharp shoes
that hurt my toes.

A false fin de siecle decorum
snored over Buenos Aires
lost in the pampas
and run by the barracks.

All day I read about newspaper coups d'état
of the leaden, internecine generals—
lumps of dough on the chessboard—and never saw
their countermarching tanks.

Along the sunlit cypress walks
of the Republican martyrs' graveyard,
hundreds of one-room Roman temples
hugged their neo-classical catafalques.

Literal commemorative busts
preserved the frogged coats
and fussy, furrowed foreheads
of those soldier bureaucrats.

By their brazen doors
a hundred marble goddesses
wept like willows. I found rest
by cupping a soft palm to each hard breast.

I was the worse for wear,
and my breath whitened the winter air
next morning, when Buenos Aires filled
with frowning, starch-collared crowds.

Dropping South: Brazil

Walking and walking in a mothy robe,
one finger pushing through the pocket-hole,
I crossed the reading room and met my soul,
hunched, spinning downward on the colored globe.
The ocean was the old Atlantic still,
always the swell greened in, rushed white, and fell,
now warmer than the air. However, there
red flags forbade our swimming. No one swam.
A lawless gentleness. The Latin blonde,
two strips of ribbon, ripened in the sun,
sleeping alone and pillowed on one arm.
No competition. Only rings of boys
butted a ball to keep it in the air,
while inland, people starved, and struck, and died—
unhappy Americas, ah *tristes tropiques!*
and nightly in the gouges by the tide,
macumba candles courted *Yemanjá*,
tall, white, the fish-tailed Virgin of the sea,
corpselike with calla lilies, walking
the water in her white night gown. "I am falling.
Santa Maria, pray for me, I want to stop,
but I have lost my foothold on the map,
now falling, falling, bent, intense, my feet
breaking my clap of thunder on the street."

Soft Wood

(FOR HARRIET WINSLOW)

Sometimes I have supposed seals
must live as long as the Scholar Gypsy.
Even in their barred pond at the zoo they are happy,
and no sunflower turns
more delicately to the sun
without a wincing of the will.

Here too in Maine things bend to the wind forever.
After two years away, one must get used
to the painted soft wood staying bright and clean,
to the air blasting an all-white wall whiter,
as it blows through curtain and screen
touched with salt and evergreen.

The green juniper berry spills crystal-clear gin,
and even the hot water in the bathtub
is more than water,
and rich with the scouring effervescence
of something healing,
the illimitable salt.

Things last, but sometimes for days here
only children seem fit to handle children,
and there is no utility or inspiration
in the wind smashing without direction.
The fresh paint
on the captains' houses hides softer wood.

Their square-riggers used to whiten
the four corners of the globe,

but it's no consolation to know
the possessors seldom outlast the possessions,
once warped and mothered by their touch.
Shed skin will never fit another wearer.

Yet the seal pack will bark past my window
summer after summer.
This is the season
when our friends may and will die daily.
Surely the lives of the old
are briefer than the young.

Harriet Winslow, who owned this house,
was more to me than my mother.
I think of you far off in Washington,
breathing in the heat wave
and air-conditioning, knowing
each drug that numbs alerts another nerve to pain.

New York 1962: Fragment

(FOR E.H.L.)

This might be nature—twenty stories high,
two water tanks, tanned shingle, corsetted
by stapled pasture wire, while bed to bed,
we two, one cell here, lie
gazing into the ether's crystal ball,
sky and a sky, and sky, and sky, till death—
my heart stops . . .
This might be heaven. Years ago,
we aimed for less and settled for
a picture, out of style then and now in,
of seven daffodils. We watched them blow:
buttercup yellow were the flowers, and green
the stems as fresh paint, over them the wind,
the blousy wooden branches of the elms,
high summer in the breath that overwhelms
the termites digging in the underpinning . . .
Still over us, still in parenthesis,
this sack of hornets sopping up the flame,
still over us our breath,
sawing and pumping to the terminal,
and down below, we two, two in one waterdrop
vitalised by a needle drop of blood,
up, up, up, up and up,
soon shot, soon slugged into the overflow
that sets the wooden workhorse working here below.

The Flaw

A seal swims like a poodle through the sheet
of blinding salt. A country graveyard, here
and there a rock, and here and there a pine,
throbs on the essence of the gasoline.
Some mote, some eye-flaw, wobbles in the heat,
hair-thin, hair-dark, the fragment of a hair—

a noose, a question? All is possible;
if there's free will, it's something like this hair,
inside my eye, outside my eye, yet free,
airless as grace, if the good God . . . I see.
Our bodies quiver. In this rustling air,
all's possible, all's unpredictable.

Old wives and husbands! Look, their gravestones wait
in couples with the names and half the date—
one future and one freedom. In a flash,
I see us whiten into skeletons,
our eager, sharpened cries, a pair of stones,
cutting like shark-fins through the boundless wash.

Two walking cobwebs, almost bodiless,
crossed paths here once, kept house, and lay in beds.
Your fingertips once touched my fingertips
and set us tingling through a thousand threads.
Poor pulsing *Fête Champêtre!* The summer slips
between our fingers into nothingness.

We too lean forward, as the heat waves roll
over our bodies, grown insensible,

ready to dwindle off into the soul,
two motes or eye-flaws, the invisible . . .
Hope of the hopeless launched and cast adrift
on the great flaw that gives the final gift.

Dear Figure curving like a questionmark,
how will you hear my answer in the dark?

Night Sweat

Work-table, litter, books and standing lamp,
plain things, my stalled equipment, the old broom—
but I am living in a tidied room,
for ten nights now I've felt the creeping damp
float over my pajamas' wilted white . . .
Sweet salt embalms me and my head is wet,
everything streams and tells me this is right;
my life's fever is soaking in night sweat—
one life, one writing! But the downward glide
and bias of existing wrings us dry—
always inside me is the child who died,
always inside me is his will to die—
one universe, one body . . . in this urn
the animal night sweats of the spirit burn.

Behind me! You! Again I feel the light
lighten my leaded eyelids, while the gray
skulled horses whinny for the soot of night.
I dabble in the dapple of the day,
a heap of wet clothes, seamy, shivering,
I see my flesh and bedding washed with light,
my child exploding into dynamite,
my wife . . . your lightness alters everything,
and tears the black web from the spider's sack,
as your heart hops and flutters like a hare.
Poor turtle, tortoise, if I cannot clear
the surface of these troubled waters here,
absolve me, help me, Dear Heart, as you bear
this world's dead weight and cycle on your back.

For the Union Dead

"Relinquunt Omnia Servare Rem Publicam."

The old South Boston Aquarium stands
in a Sahara of snow now. Its broken windows are boarded.
The bronze weathervane cod has lost half its scales.
The airy tanks are dry.

Once my nose crawled like a snail on the glass;
my hand tingled
to burst the bubbles
drifting from the noses of the cowed, compliant fish.

My hand draws back. I often sigh still
for the dark downward and vegetating kingdom
of the fish and reptile. One morning last March,
I pressed against the new barbed and galvanized

fence on the Boston Common. Behind their cage,
yellow dinosaur steamshovels were grunting
as they cropped up tons of mush and grass
to gouge their underworld garage.

Parking spaces luxuriate like civic
sandpiles in the heart of Boston.
A girdle of orange, Puritan-pumpkin colored girders
braces the tingling Statehouse,

shaking over the excavations, as it faces Colonel Shaw
and his bell-cheeked Negro infantry
on St. Gaudens' shaking Civil War relief,
propped by a plank splint against the garage's earthquake.

63

Two months after marching through Boston,
half the regiment was dead;
at the dedication,
William James could almost hear the bronze Negroes breathe.

Their monument sticks like a fishbone
in the city's throat.
Its Colonel is as lean
as a compass-needle.

He has an angry wrenlike vigilance,
a greyhound's gentle tautness;
he seems to wince at pleasure,
and suffocate for privacy.

He is out of bounds now. He rejoices in man's lovely,
peculiar power to choose life and die—
when he leads his black soldiers to death,
he cannot bend his back.

On a thousand small town New England greens,
the old white churches hold their air
of sparse, sincere rebellion; frayed flags
quilt the graveyards of the Grand Army of the Republic.

The stone statues of the abstract Union Soldier
grow slimmer and younger each year—
wasp-waisted, they doze over muskets
and muse through their sideburns . . .

Shaw's father wanted no monument
except the ditch,
where his son's body was thrown
and lost with his "niggers."

The ditch is nearer.
There are no statues for the last war here;
on Boylston Street, a commercial photograph
shows Hiroshima boiling

over a Mosler Safe, the "Rock of Ages"
that survived the blast. Space is nearer.
When I crouch to my television set,
the drained faces of Negro school-children rise like balloons.

Colonel Shaw
is riding on his bubble,
he waits
for the blessèd break.

The Aquarium is gone. Everywhere,
giant finned cars nose forward like fish;
a savage servility
slides by on grease.